Happiness: Understandings, Narratives and Discourses

Happiness: Understandings, Narratives and Discourses

Laura Hyman
University of Portsmouth, UK

First published 2014 by
PALGRAVE MACMILLAN

Palgrave Macmillan in the UK is an imprint of Macmillan Publishers Limited,
registered in England, company number 785998, of Houndmills, Basingstoke,
Hampshire RG21 6XS.

Palgrave Macmillan in the US is a division of St Martin's Press LLC,
175 Fifth Avenue, New York, NY 10010.

Palgrave Macmillan is the global academic imprint of the above companies
and has companies and representatives throughout the world.

Palgrave® and Macmillan® are registered trademarks in the United States,
the United Kingdom, Europe and other countries.

ISBN 978–1–137–32152–7

This book is printed on paper suitable for recycling and made from fully
managed and sustained forest sources. Logging, pulping and manufacturing
processes are expected to conform to the environmental regulations of the
country of origin.

A catalogue record for this book is available from the British Library.

A catalog record for this book is available from the Library of Congress.

Contents

Preface

This is a book about happiness; its title and cover makes that very clear. Why is a book on happiness important? One of the reasons why I have written this is because it occupies such a central place in contemporary British and Western societies. Almost all of us will have felt happy at various points during our lives. Listen to any pop song or read any novel, and there is a reasonable chance that happiness will feature somewhere in the words. Watch, look at or listen to any advertisement, and you will likely come across a product or service that promises to improve your life in some way. We are constantly exposed to images of a happy life, and we are also surrounded by suggested routes that we can take in order to attempt to obtain one. Not only have we seen a proliferation of the self-help book industry in recent decades, but we also have available to us a range of websites, videos and mobile phone apps that can help to guide us in the direction of happiness and fulfilment. And if that is not enough, the growth in popularity of techniques such as yoga, mindfulness and meditation in recent years means that we can be taken there by qualified experts through a vast range of classes and workshops that are now on offer. Even politicians are taking an interest in the happiness and well-being of their citizens, as we move into a fourth year of the UK government's 'Measuring National Well-Being' programme since its initial launch late in 2010. So, if happiness is such a concern to people, both in Britain and beyond, then surely it is necessary to try and understand what this thing is that seems to be preoccupying them?

In recent decades, we have witnessed a burgeoning of academic and popular psychology and self-help literature that has had an emphasis on happiness. Thus, one could ask whether this need to understand happiness has already been addressed. Well, to a degree, it has. We are now exposed to a wealth of information about the brain functions that are required to experience it, and the mental, emotional and physical techniques that individuals can engage in to bring about increased feelings of happiness. However, what seems to be missing from this branch of knowledge is an idea of how our experiences and perceptions of happiness are socially situated. That is, how do cultural and social norms, social networks and other facets of our everyday lives affect the way we experience and make sense of happiness? It is not simply a private feeling brought about on an individual, physiological level, but it also has a social context. And it is this that this book considers.

So why such a preoccupation with happiness? How and why has it become such a talking point in British society? Zygmunt Bauman's 'liquid modernity' argument (2000) could provide one answer to these questions. It could be argued that, due to increased rates of geographical mobility and fragmentation of communities, our relationships and friendships have become more fragile as our places in the world as individuals are less certain and 'fixed' than ever before. As a result, we are encouraged to be self-sufficient, and part of this self-sufficiency is a focus on the achievement of individual happiness. However, this conflicts with debates about the ways in which our class, gender, race, sexuality or place in social space *restrict* our abilities to draw on resources to make ourselves happy, which such a 'liquid modernity' perspective seems to overlook. Yet in a neoliberal and individualistic society like ours, it is this way of thinking that seems to drive dominant conceptions of happiness and our capacities to attain it.

This book is not a self-help manual, per se. I cannot guarantee that readers will be able to positively transform themselves into a state of well-being by reading it, and I apologise to anybody who bought this book in the hope that it could teach them *how* to be happy. Instead, its primary aim is to begin to fill what I feel is a gaping hole in sociological inquiry and scholarship, by providing an understanding of the ways in which people's experiences and perceptions of happiness are socially and culturally patterned. Thus far, sociologists have not fully embraced studies of happiness (and I suggest some reasons for this in the book), and those who have have largely focused upon its measurement, rather than on deeper understandings of its nature. I therefore hope that readers will nevertheless be able to take some happiness from this, by strengthening their understanding of the social framework within which it is experienced. For sociologists and non-sociologists alike, this – I hope – could also allow for a better understanding of one's own thoughts and experiences of happiness.

This book follows a number of people, through their own personal accounts of their experiences and perceptions of happiness and unhappiness, provided in interviews that I carried out. Their voices and their accounts are a central element of the book, and tell a key part of the story of how we can understand happiness in modern Britain. I explore these accounts through a distinctively sociological lens, but my intention is that they also add a dimension of real life to the book, which I hope that readers will be able to relate to. I enjoyed writing this book, and I hope that you – as readers – will enjoy reading it.

Acknowledgements

There are several people to whom I would like to offer thanks. Paul Johnson, Jane Fielding and Geoff Cooper, all at the University of Surrey, UK, provided me with invaluable advice, guidance, feedback and suggestions whilst I was undertaking the research on which this book is based. I also owe thanks to Susie Scott at the University of Sussex, UK. I am extremely grateful to all of those who took part in the interviews that formed part of the research, as without their insightful accounts of happiness, this book would not exist. I would like to thank my colleagues on the Sociology team at the University of Portsmouth – in particular, Kay Peggs, Barry Smart, Simon Stewart and Joseph Burridge have generously offered me their support and wisdom both before and during the writing process. I am lucky to have had the opportunity to work with Mark Cieslik and Alexandra Jugureanu, my fellow co-convenors of the British Sociological Association's Happiness Study Group. Thank you both for keeping me so inspired about pursuing happiness within academia. Thanks also to Beth O'Leary at Palgrave Macmillan, for her patience with my delivery of the book manuscript.

Lastly, thanks to my parents, Sandra Hyman and Richard Hyman, for all of their love, support and understanding, and to Gerard Harrison, for putting up with me and for making me happy.

1
Introduction

> The concept of happiness is such an indeterminate one that
> even though everyone wishes to attain happiness, yet he can
> never say definitely and consistently what it is that he really
> wishes and wills.
>
> (Kant, 1785/1981:27)

It could be argued that the idea of happiness is ubiquitous in contemporary Western societies such as Europe and North America; it features heavily in popular culture, advertising and mass media more broadly, and it is something that most people would feel is an inevitable goal that they strive to achieve in their lives. Many would feel that it is the pursuit of happiness that stands as the guiding principle of people's lives; indeed, as the American Declaration of Independence (1776) states, the rights of all men are 'life, liberty and the pursuit of happiness'. Although happiness is a ubiquitous aspiration, Kant's words presented here may have some relevance in the contemporary world; happiness is far from straightforward, and many people may be unable to clearly articulate the specific source and nature of their happiness. On the other hand, it being such a major facet of popular culture and human existence in this way may nevertheless leave people well-placed to be able to articulate and talk about the ways in which they experience and perceive happiness.

This book has been written at a time when happiness and wellbeing are high up on the agendas of national governments worldwide. Indeed, in November 2010, it was announced by the UK Prime Minister, David Cameron, that the United Kingdom's 'subjective

1

well-being' is to be measured on a regular basis, as part of the Office for National Statistics' (ONS) 'Measuring National Well-Being' programme. Data are collected periodically from around 165,000 respondents, as part of their Annual Population Survey, and it is hoped that this will play a key role in government policymaking, as well as providing a metric that can be used as an indicator of societal progress (for more information and results, see Office for National Statistics, 2014). This is also being undertaken by other national governments, such as France, the United States and Bhutan. It is felt that, in line with economists' findings on the relationship between happiness and wealth (which I discuss in more detail in Chapter 2), measures of well-being offer a more 'subjective' alternative to monetary, 'objective' measures of progress that are not always reflective of how people feel about their lives.

Whether or not we embrace or approve of the idea of happiness and well-being data being used to monitor national progress, it is clear that happiness plays a prominent role in the way that societies are organised. It also has a strong presence within print and broadcast media. The frequency at which articles and stories on the topic, appealing to the general public, are publicised is another indicator of the increased preoccupation that many sectors of society have with the concept of happiness. For instance, articles entitled 'Happiness and Well-Being Trump Material Growth' (Richardson, 2014) and 'Happiness Is Good for Your Health, So What Are Councils Doing about It?' (Fearn, 2014) were published in the *Guardian* in April 2014, within a period of ten days; stories of a similar nature are reported via other news outlets on an equally regular basis.

Happiness seems also to be unavoidable within popular and public discourse. Mental health charities 'Mind' and 'Rethink Mental Illness' established the 'Time to Change' campaign in 2007, the aim of which was to 'end the discrimination that surrounds mental health' (Time to Change, 2014). The campaign acknowledged that there is a stigma attached to mental illness, including depression and anxiety, and that there is a need to eradicate this. The campaign continues to be ongoing, and their website includes stories from sufferers of depression who express feelings of embarrassment and shame about their situation. There therefore continues to exist a societal pressure to appear happy and contented – and appearing happy is perhaps what we have come to understand as 'normal'. Indeed, we are frequently presented

Discourses and narratives

One way of understanding how people articulate their ideas about happiness is to examine the discourses within which they position themselves when doing so, and this is the approach that this book takes. The term 'discourse' is used to refer to the notion of it that Michel Foucault uses in his work. In a discussion of what discourse is, he states that 'alongside everything a society can produce (alongside: that is to say, in a determinate relationship with) there is the formation and transformation of "things said"' (Foucault, 1991:63). A discourse is made up of *statements* and is based upon a set of rules that prescribe which speech acts are to have meaning. It is these rules that are the main focus of Foucault's notion of discourse, rather than the language that is used, or the psyches of the human subjects who carry out the speech acts (Foucault, 1991). These rules, Foucault argues, are specific to time periods and societies, and they determine a number of things, including what it is possible to say and to talk about (as well as what it is possible to say in particular domains); which utterances are likely to be remembered for long periods of history and which may be more quickly forgotten; and *who* is likely to have access to certain discourses (that is, do certain groups or classes have better access than others?) (Foucault, 1972). However, discourses are not necessarily fixed or static; they can change if and when new utterances are added to them. Multiple discourses can also be employed simultaneously, depending upon what is being expressed through them. If and when this is the case, different discourses can compete with one another, creating tensions in people's thoughts or accounts. They are, furthermore, not things that are controlled by powerful beings; instead, 'discoursing subjects form a part of the discursive field' (Foucault, 1991:58). That is, they are not simply pre-existing structures that subjects – or people – 'use', but they are also formations that people themselves create and change, when new utterances are added. Foucault also stresses that the study of discourse is not about seeking to understand their hidden or underlying meanings, but to understand their actual form and appearance, as well as the field or conditions in which they are used or deployed. Every time period is characterised by a number of dominant discourses, which people situate themselves in, in order to make sense of their lives and the social world, to accord them with meaning. It is discourse itself that allows people to understand what is 'sayable' at each particular time point in history (Foucault, 1972, 1991). Indeed, happiness is one aspect of people's lives that is understood through a range of dominant discourses. Rather than simply being a 'private', internal experience, happiness is something that is shaped, interpreted and articulated via culturally specific ways of thinking, being and acting (Jackson, 1999). Furthermore, it could even be argued that the way in which people talk about happiness, and the way in which they position themselves within discourses of it is 'a means by which we participate in creating a shared sense' (1999:101) of what happiness is.

So, what are the discourses that people position themselves in when they are making sense of what happiness is, and how they experience it? Do people tend to use a set of dominant discourses, which together illuminate the shared or common ways in which happiness is understood in contemporary Britain? The discourses that people commonly situate themselves in when making sense of happiness will be explored, with reference to interviewees' accounts, in chapters 3–6. The term 'narrative' will also be employed to refer to something similar; in the same way that people can construct, but also make use of available narratives, or stories, about their own experiences of love (Jackson, 1993), experiences of happiness can also be articulated and made sense of via narrative. These are often shared and are one way in which we can start to examine the ways in which happiness is socially patterned.

Outline of the book

Chapter 2 sets the scene of the book by grounding it in a range of scholarly debates on happiness. Sociological literature on happiness is, as already discussed, rather scarce, but the chapter focuses on work that has been done by economists and psychologists that is often placed under the heading 'the science of happiness'. This largely focuses upon its measurement and determinants. The idea that increases in wealth are not partnered by increases in happiness is introduced here, as a rationale for needing measures of it as 'subjective' indicators of social progress. Some of the key determinants of happiness that have been put forward by scholars working in this area are also highlighted. The chapter also examines a range of sociological works, underlining the social aspects of happiness, and explaining the ways in which it can be understood as both an aspect of selfhood and identity, and an emotion.

Chapter 3 explores what people understand happiness to be, doing so through the analysis of interviewees' accounts. They positioned themselves in a range of different discourses when articulating what happiness is to them, and two broad ideas are considered; firstly, that happiness is understood to be characterised by an essentiality, rendering it immune and resistant to social factors, and secondly, that it is located within a complex normative framework whereby cultural guidelines prescribe specific ways in which happiness ought to be displayed and experienced.

The focus of Chapter 4 is the role that 'therapeutic discourse' occupies in people's accounts of happiness. This is a discourse that frames people's experiences of it, and, after explaining what it is about, I demonstrate how ideas surrounding the self and the individual are commonly regarded as being fundamental for happiness; that is, that happiness is largely constructed as a subjective, personal experience, the attainment of which is the responsibility of the individual, rather than anyone or anything else. Furthermore, the chapter also delineates the ways in which this discourse is related to a distinctive vocabulary and way of thinking that has become widely adopted amongst British people and others in the West.

Chapter 5 sets out some of the ways in which people understand the significance of interpersonal relationships for happiness. These are indeed regarded as extremely important, and, by the same token, loneliness is highlighted as a major source of *un*happiness. However, a tension emerges as this idea has been found to *compete* with tenets of therapeutic discourse, explored in Chapter 4; on one hand, an individual is expected to be solely responsible for his or her own happiness, but on the other, relationships are crucial for a happy life. This tension is considered in detail here.

Chapter 6 examines the relationship between happiness and money and working life, which were two of the 'determinants' of happiness highlighted by other scholars (discussed in Chapter 2). People not only recognised money and work as important factors in a happy life, but also positioned themselves within therapeutic discourse in their accounts of this importance. With regard to work, fulfilment was acknowledged as fundamental for job satisfaction, and with regard to money, people positioned themselves as *distinct* or different from an 'other' who may choose to spend money on expensive consumer goods (and draw happiness from this), claiming that money cannot actually 'buy' happiness.

Chapter 7 brings together the book's key conclusions and reflects upon the sociological understanding of happiness that has been offered throughout. It considers some of the ways in which the application of a sociological lens to happiness and well-being could inform and be useful for government policymaking. The chapter ends with an appeal to sociologists for greater acknowledgement of happiness in their work.

2
Happiness: The Story So Far

Happiness is a contested idea, and it is this that this book seeks to explore, via a sociological analysis of a range of lay accounts surrounding the issue. However, before these accounts are presented and examined, the scene must be set. This chapter thus delineates a number of scholarly debates within which this book, and the study on which it is based, can be framed. As highlighted in the book's Introduction, there exists a relative paucity of sociological work on happiness. That which has been undertaken tends either to focus mainly upon its measurement and determinants, rather than what it is understood to *be*, which is the focus of this book, or simply regards happiness as an outcome of other social phenomena (such as relationships or work) without necessarily examining it in detail. This, on the one hand, poses a problem as far as this book is concerned, as it cannot be easily placed within an existing academic context. However, on the other hand, it paves the way for this book to act as a pioneering work on the study of lay perceptions and understandings of happiness. I shall therefore demonstrate how ideas presented in this book *complement* those that are already known in both sociology and beyond, and how they can address and begin to fill this lacuna that has hitherto been overlooked. That is, if happiness is something that can be measured, as many debates suggest, then how is it initially experienced and brought about? Do people seek and experience happiness from the determinants, or sources, that have been highlighted in these scholarly works? The chapter shall begin with a brief discussion of the contribution to happiness studies of philosophy, particularly classical Greek philosophers such as Plato and Aristotle, and later branches of philosophy, such as utilitarianism. It shall then examine, in perhaps a rather piecemeal way, social scientific debates on happiness from the past 40 years from disciplines such as Economics and Psychology (which are often grouped under the heading of the 'science of happiness', with a focus upon its measurement and maximisation), before considering sociological work on emotion, the self and, of course, happiness itself.

Happiness and philosophy

Scholarly studies of happiness are by no means new. Plato, in *The Republic* (380 BC/1998) wrote about the way in which a balanced soul which is free of any conflict is central to the idea of happiness or *eudaimonia* (a Greek word meaning 'flourishing'). Having this means that happiness – or a state of absolute peace, joy and contentment – can be achieved. For Plato, one way in which happiness can be achieved is by acquiring the virtue of justice, where each part of the human soul is working in harmony. Having such a soul would prevent any *external* or material circumstances from allowing a person to lose their inner composure. Happiness for Plato can also be achieved through the practice of philosophy, or by contemplating the world of 'being'; this is eternal, in contrast to the impermanence of aspects of the physical world. In both cases then, happiness is achieved when an individual achieves internal balance and harmony. Whilst it could be suggested that modern conceptions of happiness differ from those of Plato, I argue here that the ideas of inner balance and harmony remain very relevant. In subsequent chapters of this book, I shall document the ways in which many people make sense of happiness as something internal, private and subjective, and that to draw happiness from aspects of the physical world (such as money, or medicine) is not 'right' or 'authentic'. This, as well as whether any other dimensions of Plato's work resonate with the discourses used by people in producing their accounts of their own experiences and perceptions of happiness, will be explored in chapters 3–6 of the book.

Aristotle – a pupil of Plato's – also wrote about happiness and stated that it is intimately related to virtue (350 BC/1998). Like Plato, he used *eudaimonia* to refer to happiness. This he related more to the idea of flourishing, which, rather than an emotional state, is about fulfilling one's potential and being a virtuous and good person. Virtue, for

Aristotle, can be achieved by having a balance between excesses and deficiencies of things. For example, central to virtue is courage – a balance between rashness and cowardice – and generosity – a balance between wastefulness and miserliness. In other words, it is moderation, rather than extremes, that is important for the achievement of *eudaimonia*. Again, the relevance of this to the discourses that people used to articulate their own experiences and perceptions of happiness in modern society will be explored in later chapters of this book.

Another branch of philosophy that is concerned with happiness is Utilitarianism, the main proponents of which were Jeremy Bentham and his student, John Stuart Mill. Established in the eighteenth century, utilitarianism was an ethical theory that placed emphasis upon the overall 'good' of society, and promoted policies and behaviours that brought about 'the greatest good for the greatest number of people' (Bentham, 1789/2009). Bentham devised a 'felicific calculus' based on a number of variables in order to calculate the level of pleasure or 'good' that an action or a policy would bring about. The higher the level, the more morally 'right' it was considered to be. Mill also adopted the 'greatest happiness principle' (1863/2001), and, like Bentham, saw acts that brought about the greatest 'good' as the most moral. However, whilst Bentham does not favour any particular form of happiness over another, Mill argues that intellectual and moral pleasures are superior to physical ones. He also distinguishes between 'higher' and 'lower' forms of happiness, suggesting that people who have not experienced 'high culture' are only able to experience 'lower' forms of happiness, or 'simple pleasures'. Understanding happiness, or utility, in relation to policies that can benefit large numbers of people is an idea that is strongly adopted by economists of happiness, as will be shown later in the next section of this chapter. This is clearly relevant to conceptions of happiness today – especially as this idea underpins the UK government's initiatives for measuring and addressing well-being. However, an understanding of everyday experiences of happiness at a 'micro' level is needed to complete this picture, and it is this that this book seeks to do.

The science of happiness

Much of the social scientific work that has been undertaken during the past 40 years or so has been focused on the measurement and determinants of happiness, and is commonly known as the 'science of happiness'. It has been not only mainly led by economists like Richard Easterlin (1974) and Richard Layard (2011), but also enhanced by 'positive' psychologists such as Martin Seligman (2002) and Daniel Kahneman (Kahneman, Diener and Schwarz, 1999), who promote a psychology of positive human functioning. Such scholars seek to emphasise and promote positive emotion and human strengths and virtues, rather than psychology's more traditional focus of suffering and mental illness (Seligman, 2002). The general idea that all such happiness research is based on is that measures of happiness are now necessary as 'social indicators' in order to monitor societal well-being and progress, as an alternative to more traditional economic measures such as gross domestic product (GDP); these are no longer adequate predictors of subjective well-being (Easterlin, 1974, Layard, 2011, Oswald, 1997). In line with this idea, economist Richard Easterlin has argued that, since the Second World War, although people who are high earners are generally happier than those who are low earners, increases in income or national wealth have not always been partnered by an increase in happiness (an idea known as the 'Easterlin Paradox'). Thus, such economists and psychologists have done extensive work on uncovering the determinants of happiness, with a view that increased happiness (and thus an increase of the determinants of it) will lead to increased progress. It is in this way that happiness research can influence public policy.

Social indicators, a concept developed in the United States in the 1960s, can be defined as statistics that are used to measure societal conditions at a given time, in a given place. Raymond Bauer, perceived by many as the 'founding father' of the 'social indicators movement' defined the concept as follows:

> Social indicators [can be defined as] statistics, statistical series, and all other forms of evidence that enable us to assess where we stand and where we are going with respect to our values and goals.
>
> (Bauer, 1966:1)

Happiness measures are increasingly being utilised as subjective social indicators, with which societal conditions and progress can be monitored. This process rests upon the theoretical assumption that happiness is intimately linked with the 'goals and values' of a society.

These statistics – on a local, national or international level – can serve as a complement to the existing economic or objective social indicators (such as GDP, unemployment rates and crime rates) that have traditionally been used by many national governments for this purpose. It has been assumed that high levels of happiness represent societal progress, and a need to monitor such progress acts as a rationale for generating national measures of happiness. It is this recent interest in happiness as a measure of progress that has fuelled much of scholars' interest in the study of it.

An increasing number of economists and psychologists have undertaken quantitative analyses of the determinants of happiness, using a variable that is derived from a 'global' happiness question that has been implemented in several large-scale social surveys, such as the European Social Survey, the British Social Attitudes Survey and the British Household Panel Survey. Such a question asks: *Taking all things together, how happy would you say you are with your life?* Respondents would then be required to rate their happiness levels using a Likert scale consisting of a number of points (usually 3, 5 or 11). Other methods, utilised by psychologists, have focused upon gathering more detailed responses; the Experience Sampling Method (ESM) (Csikszentmihalyi and Hunter, 2003) involves participants being provided with a mobile device for a given period and responding to its 'beeps' at various points throughout each day, by providing answers to questions about how they are feeling at that moment. A less intrusive variant of this, known as the Day Reconstruction Method (DSM) (Kahneman et al., 2004), asks respondents to divide up the previous day into 'episodes' and then recall what they were doing and how they were feeling during each one. Though these obviously yield more detailed data, they can be problematic as methods, as they rest on the assumption that the happiness and enjoyment people feel moment-to-moment can be aggregated to represent how they feel about their lives overall, whereas the former and the latter may be two distinct things, as I will outline later in this chapter.

Economist Richard Layard (2011) has highlighted seven main 'causes' of happiness, derived from analyses of statistical happiness data, from the American General Social Survey (GSS): family and marriage relationships, financial situation, work (and the meaning and fulfilment it provides people with), community and friendship networks, health, personal freedom and personal values. Each of these seven causes of happiness featured as variables in the GSS, and with regard to the first five, respondents were asked to report their happiness levels in each of these domains of life. Personal freedom was captured through a variable measuring 'quality of government', particularly with regard to the unhappiness that has been found to be associated with Communist societies, in which there is a lack of freedom (Layard, 2011). Personal values, or an ability to 'discipline' one's mind, were captured through a variable measuring the self-reported importance of God in an individual's life. Layard ranked the first five causes in order of 'importance', based on the happiness ratings assigned by respondents to each. Personal freedom and values were not ranked in the same way because these were measured using a different scale. Indeed, much of the work undertaken by social scientists that forms part of this body of work known as the 'science of happiness' also highlights many of the above factors as causes of happiness (see Easterlin, 2001, Gardner and Oswald, 2002, Helliwell and Putnam, 2004, Oswald, 1997, for example).

A number of different initiatives have been proposed that could be implemented to make societies happier. These are promoting intrinsic motivation at work, promoting work–life balance, tightening controls on advertising, a redistribution of wealth through higher taxation, promoting social capital by reducing geographical mobility and promoting mental health through higher investment in psychotherapy (Layard, 2011). Some, though not all, of these have begun to be implemented in Britain; in particular, well-being at work programmes and work–life balance are encouraged by Action for Happiness, the 'movement for positive social change' that Layard founded along with colleagues Geoff Mulgan and Anthony Seldon (Action for Happiness, 2014). However, adoption of many of these may not necessarily be straightforward. For instance, many people may be unable or unwilling to work fewer hours, and geographical mobility may be difficult to reduce, particularly when jobs are difficult to come by in one's own locality (Thin, 2012). Furthermore, psychotherapy may not be an appropriate method for increasing happiness levels; not only might some people be unwilling to undergo it, but it has also been argued by sociologists that such therapies result in a *medicalisation*, which individualises problems that are actually social in nature (Shaw and Taplin, 2007). In other words, problems that are social structural in nature (such as declining community cohesion) are addressed with individual-level solutions.

Nevertheless, the determinants that have been put forward by Layard and other scholars certainly have a great deal of relevance in people's experiences of happiness. This book focuses specifically on the first four factors outlined by Layard – family relationships, financial situation, work and community and friendship networks – and, in chapters 5 and 6, examines their presence in people's qualitative narratives of happiness. Health did not feature as heavily in people's accounts of happiness as these four factors, and thus, for this reason, it was decided that it would not feature as a key theme of the book. The themes of personal freedom and personal values are drawn upon throughout. However, it must be emphasised here that whilst these factors do indeed feature heavily in lay accounts of happiness, the way in which they do so is not as linear or straightforward as many scholars working in this area suggest. This book demonstrates the ways in which these factors play out in everyday lived experiences of happiness, thus complementing that which is already known about the relationship that happiness has with them. More particularly, what Layard does not acknowledge with regard to the factor of 'personal freedom' is subjective, or a self-identified sense of freedom; one thing that this book highlights (in accordance with a number of other studies: see Rose 1996 and Furedi 2004 for examples) is that individuals are likely to experience more happiness if they feel that they have autonomy and control over their own everyday lives. This is a theme that is particularly central to this book, and will be explored further in latter sections. The sociological, cultural understanding of happiness that this book seeks to offer in relation to these factors at the level of everyday experience can problematise, but also complement the picture of happiness provided by scholars of the 'science of happiness'. That is, on the one hand, it can serve as a reminder that work of this sort does not raise questions about what happiness *is*; it assumes that it is a goal which the majority of people wish to achieve, that it is something which is measurable and quantifiable, and that it can be captured by asking people for assessments of how they feel. However, on the other, gaining a sociological understanding of what people understand happiness to be, and how they experience it can assist in addressing these questions that hitherto remain unanswered.

Social happiness?

At the heart of this book lies the idea that happiness is a social experience. Whilst it is commonly regarded in Western societies as something individual, subjective and private (and this idea will be explored in more detail in the next few chapters), our happiness can also be shaped, experienced and interpreted through social and cultural processes that are located in the world around us, outside our selves. It is more than evident from studies undertaken by economists and psychologists (outlined in the previous section) that factors such as relationships, working life and money play a part in these processes, but *how* do they help to channel happiness and well-being? We already know that they are key determinants of it, but one can go further in seeking to understand their relationship at the level of the everyday.

Social context is extremely important for our experiences and understandings of happiness, and a number of contextual factors at a macro level can have an effect on it (Bartram, 2012). One is the quality of a country's governance; this determines the quality and quantity of services provided in a locality, which would in turn affect the way people feel about their living conditions (Frey and Stutzer, 2002). Another is people's participation in voluntary organisations; this benefits those who volunteer, as well as others, who are able to enjoy greater social cohesion (Veenhoven, 2004). A country's or society's employment situation also affects people's happiness; not only do unemployed people feel unhappy due to their lack of job prospects, but those who are employed may also experience heighted fear about the potential of losing their jobs, particularly in a recession (Di Tella et al., 2003). David Bartram (2012) also points to the importance of cultural differences, as one's culture can affect the kinds of meanings that they attach to happiness, as well as the way in which they understand it. For instance, Americans and Europeans, who are more individualist, are likely to understand happiness in a different way to East Asians, who are more collective in terms of culture. For individualists, happiness is rooted in self-esteem and individual fulfilment, whereas for collectivists, it is understood in terms of social connections and solidarity within communities (Kitayama and Markus, 2000).

Neil Thin (2012) also places emphasis on the social dimensions of happiness, and highlights a need for happiness to play a role in social policymaking. This is because, rather than being a private, subjective experience, happiness is bound up with connections and engagement in the workplace and community; that is, it is about people relating to one another. Rather than assuming that happiness is simply an *outcome* of a range of social processes (which is the case with some happiness studies scholars), Thin asserts that happiness can help to improve other areas of society, such as health, community and productivity at work. Therefore, public policies that are aimed at happiness must not only benefit the aspects of the external, wider world, but must also be recognised by individuals as having a positive impact. This is important – there is little point in external conditions being conducive to happiness if people feel unhappy in a subjective sense, and the same would go for people who felt happy but had poor living conditions. Thus, a balance between 'objective' and 'subjective' happiness is necessary. This is a particularly pertinent point, as it will be demonstrated in the next few chapters that happiness is commonly understood to be individual, and thus any policies would need to resonate with individual psyches. In order to know *what* would work in this situation, an understanding of what happiness means to people, and how they experience it, is necessary, and this is what this book seeks to provide.

Happiness works as a regulatory power in our day-to-day lives, according to Sara Ahmed (2010). She suggests that happiness is attached to particular objects, and that if one can orient themselves to such objects – which can be feelings, identifications, life choices, amongst other things – happiness is promised for the future, by any number of social actors or agencies. It is in this way that Ahmed says that there exists a 'happiness directive'. However, in attaching happiness to such objects, other 'abject' subjects and identities are excluded from narratives and scripts of happiness and success, and are instead associated with unhappiness and suffering. Ahmed gives the feminist killjoy, the unhappy queer and the melancholic migrant as examples of such identities. Whether or not Ahmed's ideas are embraced, she clearly illustrates how happiness works as a regulatory power in our day-to-day lives and it is this kind of an approach that is important here. It could be argued that this sheds light on the 'empathetic' dimensions of happiness, which tend to be overlooked by many of the 'science of happiness' scholars, but which are fundamental if we are to seek a well-rounded understanding of the place that happiness occupies in British society.

Now that we have an understanding of some of the broad ways in which happiness can be considered a social experience, I would like to draw attention to some of the intricacies surrounding the way in which happiness can be conceptualised. Readers will have noticed at this point in the book that I have not sought to arrive at a *definition* of happiness. This is deliberate, and I will not, strictly speaking, do so anywhere in the book. This is because the accounts of the people who were interviewed as part of the study on which this book is based shed light upon the complex meanings that are attached to experiences of happiness, and these should leave readers well placed to reach their own understanding of what happiness is commonly thought to be. Nevertheless, what can be borne in mind about happiness is that it can be conceptualised in two ways: as an aspect of a person's identity and selfhood, and as an emotion.

Self, identity and personhood

Happiness is inextricably bound up with the way in which people make sense of their selves and identities. Some scholars have suggested that in modernity, people in the West live their lives as though they are 'projects'. Zygmunt Bauman, who postulates the concept of 'liquid modernity', whereby traditional institutions are less fixed and can no longer be used by people as frames of reference with which to plan their lives or actions (Bauman, 2000), suggests that we now need to be 'artists of life' (2008). In other words, we must seek to give our lives purpose, by reflecting on our lives and actions. The purpose of the 'art of life', Bauman says, is happiness, and this should be sought via an individual 'life project' (2000). In a similar vein, the self has been theorised as 'reflexive'. Anthony Giddens, for instance, suggests that reflexivity is central to the development of 'life politics' where individuals seek to construct and reconstruct a biography or a narrative of self-identity throughout their life course. That is, people feel encouraged to continually reflect on their lives and events that occur, and to seek to transform their sense of self by 'moving forward', closer to the attainment of happiness (Giddens, 1991). He thus puts forward a model of the self that is both able to reflect on itself and know itself, and, as will be explored in later chapters of the book, the ability to do each of these things is fundamental to the experience of happiness for many people. Nikolas Rose articulates the idea of one's life being comparable to a 'project':

> Contemporary individuals are incited to live as if making a *project* of themselves: they are to *work* on their emotional world, their domestic and conjugal arrangements, their relations with employment and their techniques of sexual pleasure, to develop a 'style' of living that will maximise the worth of their existence to themselves. Evidence from the United States, Europe, and the United Kingdom suggests that the implantation of such 'identity projects', characteristic of advanced liberal democracies, is constitutively linked to the rise of a new breed of spiritual directors, 'engineers of the human soul'...[the activities of these figures]...promise to allow us to transform our selves in the direction of happiness and fulfilment.

> (Rose, 1996:157)

Therefore, for Rose, understanding our lives in this way allows us to develop a 'style of living' that facilitates the attainment of (or at least, aspiration towards) happiness. Whether or not the development of such a 'project' is possible for everyone is open to question; it may be that people have unequal access to the resources, practices and dispositions necessary to be an 'artist of life' as such (Skeggs, 2004). This will be considered further in Chapter 6.

The idea that one's life can be understood as a 'project', of which happiness is a fundamental part, can be linked to the growing popularity of the self-help industry in the United States and Britain in recent decades. Self-help literature advises readers about how to be happier in many different spheres of life, including in their intimate relationships, their sex life, with their children and at work; they emphasise the importance of the reader finding their 'true self' after 'overcoming' negative emotions such as fear, shame or guilt (which may have been unconsciously felt), in order that happiness can be achieved and the 'true self' can be found. The state of happiness is defined as healthy and desirable, and, rather than being viewed as a natural part of emotional experience, negative emotions are seen to be a destructive force preventing individuals from achieving happiness and in need of eradication (Illouz, 2007). The term 'self-help industry' could even be broadened and renamed the 'happiness industry', as we have not only witnessed a growing availability of self-help materials such as DVDs, websites and smartphone 'apps', but we are also being presented with advertisements for classes that are taught by 'experts', such as yoga, mindfulness and meditation, which are aimed at people who prefer to be helped by teachers rather than by themselves.

Sociologists have argued that the emergence of this industry in countries such as the United Kingdom and America is part of a broader cultural shift, called the 'therapeutic turn' (Illouz, 2008). This is 'a cultural shift from reticence and self-reliance to emotional expressiveness and help-seeking' (Wright, 2008:321), and is bound up with an increasing influence of psychology, the rise of counselling and therapy and an associated preoccupation with the self and internal life during the twentieth and twenty-first centuries. Frank Furedi (2004), for instance, argues that everyday experiences and activities are being talked and thought about in a more 'emotional' way, and that words which were previously confined to the realm of psychotherapy and psychology (or the 'psy sciences'), such as 'stress', 'anxiety', 'trauma' and 'syndrome' are now commonly appearing in our everyday vocabulary to describe not just troublesome experiences, but also those considered 'normal':

> Through pathologising negative emotional responses to the pressures of life, contemporary culture unwittingly encourages people to feel traumatised and depressed by experiences hitherto regarded as routine.
>
> (Furedi, 2004:6)

The therapeutic turn, or shift towards a 'therapy culture', characterised by an increased public recognition of personal pain, suffering and emotional experience, has essentially changed the way in which happiness is understood in modern societies. It has become something that is to be actively striven for and reflected upon; regardless of whether or not people undergo therapy or counselling, happiness is rendered a 'goal' that can be reached once negative feelings have been managed, 'worked' through and – possibly – eradicated. Nikolas Rose, in his book 'Inventing Our Selves' (1996), suggests that the behaviour of individuals living in advanced liberal democracies is centred around their desire for the maximisation of happiness and physical and mental well-being. This originates from the promotion of an image of the human being, created by the 'enterprise culture' of the late 1980s (that is still prevalent today), as being a subjective, autonomous individual who strives for personal fulfilment, with the capacity to do so via acts of choice. Taking a Foucauldian approach, Rose argues that political power is exercised *through* the promotion of this subjectivity, rather than working to suppress it (Foucault, 1982), and that this subjectivity is fundamental to procedures of regulation and governmentality. Thus, people are likely to decide to behave in ways that would induce positive emotions (like happiness) and minimise negative feeling.

Furedi (2004) asserts that 'therapeutic culture provides a script through which individuals develop a distinct understanding of their selves and of their relationship with others' (2004:23). In other words, therapy culture is considered a kind of cultural discourse or *resource* that individuals draw upon to make sense of their every-day lives and experiences. Not only are individuals provided with this 'script' with which to articulate their experiences, but they also actively work to *create* this resource or this culture that underlies their perceptions of their selves and their lives, and they learn to articulate these perceptions through producing and reproducing this therapeutic – or 'psy' – discourse. It will be shown throughout the rest of the book how people produce their accounts of happiness by positioning themselves within therapeutic discourse.

Therapeutic culture, or the 'therapeutic turn', has been theorised by a number of sociologists over the last 50 years. Much has been written on the increasing popularity of therapy and counselling as a solution to personal problems, the permeation of 'psychological' language into everyday, lay vocabulary and the increased preoccupation with the self and emotional life that Western societies have witnessed in recent years (see Bellah, 1985, Lasch, 1979, Rieff, 1966, Wright, 2008). It could also be said that this cultural turn is resulting in more people being 'in touch' with their feelings; American sociologist Robert Bellah (1985) has written about how the expansion of the realm of therapy towards the end of the twentieth century has led to a general increase in concern for monitoring, managing and expressing feelings. This is evident in the rise of the term 'emotional intelligence', popularised by psychologist Daniel Goleman (1996) after the publication of his book with the same title in the late 1990s. The term refers to 'the ability to monitor one's own and others' emotions, to discriminate among them, and to use the information to guide one's thinking and actions' (Mayer and Salovey, 1993:433). The book is now a popular bestseller in the United Kingdom and elsewhere, which suggests that this kind of culture and vocabulary is being increasingly used by many to make sense of their lives and experiences.

A key aspect of therapeutic discourse is the distinctive way in which individuals make sense of their selves. This particular constitution of the self, according to Rebecca Hazleden (2003), is adopted in self-help literature, but has permeated into everyday vocabulary. Hazleden demonstrates, through an analysis of a sample of relationship manuals, the way in which they set up a relation of the reader's self *to itself*. Such manuals, along with other self-help texts, present the self as being '*ontologically separate* from itself' (Hazleden, 2003:416). For example, Joyce Vedral, in her relationship manual, *Get Rid of Him!* (1994), advises readers:

> What is self-esteem anyway? It is your reputation with yourself – in essence, it is what, over time, you have come to believe about yourself. If you have low self-esteem, you have built up a bad reputation with yourself. If you have high self-esteem, you have built up a good reputation with yourself.
>
> (Vedral, 1994:20)

Vedral encourages readers to reflect on the reputation that they have with their selves (and indeed, other self-help authors whose texts Hazleden found to use similar language). The self, therefore, becomes the primary site on which individuals are invited to 'work'; the end result of this 'work', Hazleden says, is the individual becoming more aware of his or her 'true' self, from which they may have become separated. Awareness of this can lead to happiness, as will be shown in relation to interviewees' accounts in later chapters. Emphasis is also placed in these texts upon the importance of the individual learning to know, and furthermore, *love* his or her self. This can be done by engaging in internal dialogue with oneself, and is particularly important when one is in – or about to begin – an intimate relationship (Hazleden, 2003). Hazleden also suggests that such books advise readers that acquiring self-knowledge in this way allows them to position themselves on a desired 'life path' (2003:421) so that personal fulfilment can be achieved. She says that, according to the books, 'we are to aspire to be effective, fulfilled and autonomous selves, on an individual, progressive and linear journey through life, with the sole responsibility for the direction that this journey takes' (2003:421). One should not, therefore, rely on anybody else for this fulfilment, but rather, they should be self-sufficient in developing technologies of the self such as self-knowledge and self-love. Thus, not only is this particular constitution of the self central to therapeutic discourse used in self-help texts, but it is also key – as Hazleden shows us – to the way in which many people may seek to transform themselves into fulfilled and happy individuals (both in their relationships and otherwise).

Individuals think about their selves as 'ontologically separate' when making use of what Michel Foucault has termed 'technologies of the self', that

> permit individuals to effect by their own means or with the help of others a certain number of operations on their own bodies and souls, thoughts, conduct and way of being, so as to transform themselves in order to attain a certain state of happiness, purity, wisdom, perfection, or immortality.
>
> (Foucault, 1988:18)

Foucault explains how the notion of the 'care of the self' (1986), first used by Socrates in Greco-Roman philosophy in the first two centuries AD, lies at the centre of the 'art of existence'. This is a central tenet of therapeutic culture, and can be seen in the overwhelming popularity in the West of self-help guides, anti-depressants or even 'relaxing' leisure activities like yoga or meditation on which people draw to make themselves feel more positive or happy about life. Furthermore, the self-knowledge and self-love that can be fostered when caring for the self are also technologies in this way. It is only by regarding one's self as something ontologically separate from them as a person – which Hazelden outlines – that 'caring' for the self can take place. This can be done with the help of 'engineers of the human soul' (Rose, 1996), such as therapists, authors of self-help books or yoga instructors, who earn a living using their expertise and knowledge of human subjectivity. Thus, one could say that such technologies act as aids to emotion management (Hochschild, 1983: further discussion of this concept is provided later in this chapter) that can mask, or even eradicate negative feelings that are classed by society as undesirable, and bring about positive emotions that enhance overall quality of life. Furthermore, it is in this way that a desire for happiness can facilitate social control; a need to seek happiness and to be reasonably happy is portrayed by society as a central goal of the everyday lives of most individuals. Via a process of normalisation (Foucault, 1977), a certain level of happiness is considered desirable, healthy or 'normal' by wider society and if, for any reason, one fell below this threshold of happiness, they may be compelled or encouraged to draw on external sources (whether it be a therapist, anti-depressants, sharing 'problems' with close friends or family or so on) in order that an acceptable or 'normal' level of contentment is regained. Thus, culture 'prescribes' socially desirable behaviour that is conducive to happiness. Foucault's precept of the 'care of the self' is also a central part of the therapeutic culture that people use to make sense of their experiences of happiness; they may undertake this self-care in order to maintain or increase feelings of happiness. Individuals who are able to care for themselves in this way are considered to be more 'effective' citizens who are able to take responsibility for themselves (Hazleden, 2003, Rose, 1996).

As stated above, one way in which people may seek to care for their selves is via the self-help book; indeed, therapeutic discourse is largely used by the authors of these books in offering advice to their readers. Heidi Rimke (2000) undertook an exploration of contemporary self-help literature with regard to the way in which readers, or 'subjects', are compelled to pursue self-improvement. The self-improvement techniques that the books advise readers to engage in are closely linked with the political organisation of neoliberal societies, in that the caring for and fashioning of selves ensures that effective citizens, who are able to take responsibility for themselves, are produced (Rimke, 2000). That is, 'the self becomes an object of knowledge *and* a subject/object of governance, not simply under the gaze of an expert acting at a distance but, most importantly, under the ever-present gaze of one's self' (2000:68).

Caring for the self, and self-examination, according to Rimke, are championed by self-help texts as something that readers must strive towards in order to better themselves and to be happy (2000). They are encouraged to engage in internal dialogue and ask themselves questions in order to achieve self-improvement. These are central tenets of therapeutic discourse, and Rimke suggests that it is via such books and manuals that the discourse creates *truths* about people and the ways in which their selves and characters operate (Foucault, 1972; see Chapter 1 for further discussion of discourse). Indeed, as Foucault states, 'In the self-help tradition the examination of one's self paves the way to self-knowledge by "superimposing truth about self through memory, that is by memorizing the rules" of self-regulation' (Foucault, 1988: 43). It is in this way that therapeutic discourse creates truth about the self, and in this case, it is via the medium of the self-help text that this creation of truth is established and happiness can be achieved.

However, the therapeutic discourse that constitutes self-help literature serves to obscure the ways in which human beings are essentially interdependent and collective (Rimke, 2000). That is, self-examination, care for the self and personal autonomy are presented as essential truths in these texts, and they have come to constitute the primary, and indeed 'normal', way in which many people see themselves. The idea that this kind of self-examination may be inextricably bound up with a *social* arena (that is, the political organisation of neoliberal democracies) and not from 'inside' the self is not necessarily evident or obvious to the majority of people, for whom modes of personhood are made sense of via psychological and individual ideas.

Thus, happiness has, for many, become a major preoccupation, and to be a 'happy person' is a key aim for many people. Eva Illouz (2007) asserts that emotion has become increasingly central to the workplace; managers are encouraged to display sympathy and an ability to listen to others, and the idea of 'communication' is seen as fundamental to the everyday running of the organisation. That is, the happiness of workers is a high priority in many workplaces. Similarly, schools, colleges and universities are also placing increased emphasis upon the emotional health of pupils and students (Ecclestone and Hayes, 2009). Illouz attributes this change in culture to the passing of the 1946 National Mental Health Act in the USA; this meant that in the early 1950s, the work of psychologists began to extend to the mental health of ordinary citizens, rather than simply intense mental disorders. This led to an expansion of the market of therapeutic services, and she notes that 'by the 1960s, psychology had become fully institutionalised and had become an intrinsic aspect of American popular culture' (Illouz, 2007:25). Whilst this may have happened slightly later in the United Kingdom, it is also evident that similar changes have taken place, and that for many people in the Western world, their conceptions of happiness are underpinned by therapeutic culture and discourse.

Emotion

Happiness can also be made sense of as an emotion. It can be felt in response to events that take place in one's external environment, and can be short-term and fleeting, or longer lasting. People's emotional displays and expressions, particularly with regard to happiness, are surrounded by a framework of social norms and expectations. Sociologist of emotion Arlie Russell Hochschild (1979) asserts that culture-specific norms that are present in a society govern how an individual 'should' feel in different circumstances (that is, a feeling that is 'appropriate' to the situation). She calls these norms 'feeling rules' which are 'the social guidelines that direct how we want to try and feel' (1979:563); these rules play a major role in the 'culture of emotion' (1998:7) found in each society. Although Hochschild does not consider happiness in an explicit manner, this perspective can certainly be applied to it, inasmuch as norms and rules exist in relation to the display and feeling of happiness: an example of a feeling rule from contemporary Western culture is the norm that one 'ought' to feel happy on their wedding day as this is commonly understood to be the happiest day of one's life. But what happens if there is a discrepancy or dissonance between what an individual actually feels and what the feeling rule 'prescribes' for a given situation? Hochschild states that 'the individual often works on inducing or inhibiting feelings so as to render them "appropriate" to a situation' (1979:551). She calls this act of inducement or inhibition 'emotion work' or 'emotion management'. Therefore, a groom- or bride-to-be who feels anxious or worried about the prospect of getting married may feel compelled to display happiness to their wedding guests, in order to conform to the feeling rules attached to the situation. Similarly, emotion work is also undertaken in a number of different workplace settings; in this context, it is known as 'emotional labour' (Hochschild, 1983). Workers in service sector roles, particularly those who are client- or customer-facing, are usually expected to undertake emotional labour whilst at work. In many of these cases, staff are trained and socialised to appear happy and friendly at all times during interaction with customers and clients, irrespective of what they actually feel, in order to maintain a positive image of the company they worked for. Hochschild wrote about this in her groundbreaking book 'The Managed Heart' (1983), in relation to airline cabin crew members. It is in this way that she argues that emotion – and of course, happiness – can be 'sold for a wage'. Emotion work:

> requires one to induce or suppress feelings in order to sustain the outward countenance that produces the proper state of mind in others... This kind of labour calls for the coordination of mind and feeling, and it sometimes draws on a source of self that we honour as deep and integral to our individuality... Emotional labour... is sold for a wage and therefore has exchange value.
>
> (Hochschild, 1983:7)

Therefore culturally prescribed feeling rules and emotion management that may be undertaken as a result of such rules can strongly shape what people feel and when and how intensely they feel it; this can very often apply to the feeling and expression of happiness, whether it may be genuine or 'managed'. Not only can feeling rules constrain when, how and why happiness is experienced or displayed (for example, it is very appropriate at a wedding, but may be very inappropriate at a funeral), but they are also *produced* or created by people themselves, and it is their subsequent widespread use that renders them part of a normative framework within which happiness is located and experienced by individuals.

Happiness can also be expressed in the form of cheerfulness. Christina Kotchemidova (2005) has written about how cheerfulness became a common emotional expression from the late eighteenth century onwards, particularly in America. This corresponded with the onset of the Enlightenment, as the emergence of rationalistic tendencies brought about a stronger emphasis on taking care of oneself and pursuing happiness. Wage-earners were also expected to be happy because of their improved working conditions, and thus good cheer and humour became a sign of social responsibility (Kotchemidova, 2005). Stemming from this, happiness and cheerfulness were desirable displays as they were understood to be markers of status and high levels of control. Over the twentieth century, however, as rationality became a more dominant facet of the working world, emotionality was regarded negatively, as it was seen to be a hindrance to the controlled rationality that contributes to productivity in the workplace. Nevertheless, cheerfulness continued to be viewed as important for both consumption and production, as it is presented as the end result of the consuming of goods, and is also understood to be a characteristic of productive workers. Cheerfulness, and appearing happy, therefore became a 'national ethic' in the United States. Kotchemidova goes on to write about how cheerfulness has been commodified in post-industrial capitalist society, in both America and in many parts of Europe, as it is now a key element of the 'emotional labour' that service workers undertake when interacting with their customers (Hochschild, 1983). Not only are staff trained to be cheerful in this way, but they often put on such a display on their own accord, as they understand that customers are likely to expect cheerfulness as part of the service that they receive. The dominance of cheerfulness in Western societies, Kotchemidova argues, may have a part to play in the way that depression is understood. As cheerfulness has been 'normalised', a failure to conform to this – and to the pursuit of happiness – is regarded as a pathology, or an illness; depression. The more cheerfulness is regarded as the norm, the more depression will be seen negatively.

Therefore happiness, when understood as an emotion, can be said to be situated within a complex system of norms and rules. Not only is it surrounded by 'feeling rules' that prescribe when, to whom, and in what situations happiness should be expressed and displayed (Hochschild, 1979), but there also exist more general expectations surrounding the *level* of happiness (or cheerfulness) that it is permissible to display in public. As will be demonstrated in the proceeding chapter, the accounts of happiness provided by interviewees show a simultaneous undesirability of displaying *not enough* happiness (as would be the case with depressives) and *too much* of it (which, for reasons that will be outlined in Chapter 3, could be 'unnatural' or inauthentic). What is interesting about this is that whilst Kotchemidova's analysis implicitly suggests that limitless levels of cheerfulness are regarded as desirable in American public culture, the data provided by these British interviewees demonstrate that a *balance* must be negotiated in terms of cheerfulness and happiness displays. Whilst it is clearly preferable for individuals to appear happy rather than sad or miserable, this is only the case up to a point. Perhaps, then, the social meanings attached to emotions such as cheerfulness and happiness in British culture differ from that of America, and that emotional normative frameworks in different societies must be understood differently.

Despite this growing concern with the study of emotion, few, if any, sociologists working in this area have focused upon happiness. By way of example, the indexes of a number of key texts and edited collections on the sociology of emotion do not contain a single reference to happiness: *Emotions: A Social Science Reader* (Greco and Stenner (eds), 2008), *Emotions and Sociology* (Barbalet (ed), 2002) and *Emotions in Social Life* (Bendelow and Williams (eds), 1998). Those that do contain references tend to point to brief, and often fleeting, appearances that appear as part of a wider discussion of emotion more generally (Lupton, 1998, Turner and Stets, 2005), rather than to more explicit discussion of the relationship between happiness and social or cultural processes. Nevertheless, the sociology of emotion as a body of literature provides a useful background against which happiness can be considered, and to which it can be applied.

Understanding happiness sociologically

So happiness is by no means a straightforward concept. Some might say that it is an emotion, triggered by events or occurrences (as it is by some sociologists of emotion; see Kemper, 1984, Turner and Stets, 2005), whilst others might argue that it is a 'state of mind' and part of one's identity and selfhood. Thus, if there exists these two ideas about what happiness is, then the determinants of happiness highlighted in the 'science of happiness' literature may not necessarily impact on how happy people feel through the direct causal links that they postulate. Rather, there may be a multitude of social and cultural processes that simultaneously come into play when a person feels and experiences happiness. Thus, happiness may be more complex a phenomenon than existing research has initially assumed.

Neither of these two understandings of happiness is more 'appropriate' than the other, and both are of equal relevance. However, what this means is that happiness must be thought of as a multi-faceted phenomenon, embedded in a range of social and cultural processes. It can be both an emotion, and an aspect of selfhood, a cause and an effect of social situations or interactions, as well as something that is strongly linked to the social context by which it is surrounded. Rather than understanding happiness by imposing a narrow definition upon such an intricate concept, we can view it in this way in order that all of its complexities can be fully appreciated.

We can begin to understand happiness by examining the way in which people articulate their experiences and perceptions of it through the use of *discourse* or *narratives*. As discussed in Chapter 1, they can both be used in similar ways as analytical tools with which people's accounts of happiness can be examined and understood. Questions can now be asked: how do people organise their understandings and experiences of happiness? How do they position themselves within different discourses when articulating their accounts? And how do people select scripts from their overall repertoire with which to narrate how they think and feel? All of these questions will be explored in the pages that follow.

3
What Is Happiness?

Chapter 2 explored a range of perspectives on happiness from across a range of disciplines. What is striking about much of the existing social scientific work that has been undertaken on happiness is that questions about what happiness is understood to *be* are seemingly absent. This chapter thus presents an examination of this, in the form of a qualitative analysis of how people understand happiness. Gaining an understanding of this plays a fundamental role in the way in which we can obtain an insight into the way in which people use discourse or culturally rooted narratives in producing their accounts of their experiences and perceptions of happiness.

So what do people say that happiness *is*? How do people organise their individual experiences of it? And how do they situate themselves within particular discourses of happiness? This chapter seeks to provide an answer to the question 'what is happiness?'; a sociological understanding of what people think it is is key in making sense of its social construction.

All of the respondents who were interviewed as part of the study reflected upon what they think happiness is and positioned themselves within a range of discourses in doing so; each of these will be explored here in turn. The first concerns the idea that happiness is 'elusive'.

The elusiveness of happiness

The idea that there is no straightforward, clear-cut way in which happiness can be defined was explicitly highlighted by some of the people who were interviewed; they expressed that it might be the case that many people may not fully understand what happiness is and therefore would not know whether they felt happy or not. In other words, happiness is something *elusive*. Indeed, this is a discourse within which people have also been shown to position themselves in relation to *love*, which is commonly described as difficult to understand and 'resistant to descriptive language' (Johnson, 2005:25). Beth was one person who voiced this idea.

> Beth (23, female): I don't know if everyone has the right idea of what happiness is. Like, if you think about relationships and things like that, some people think that a particular person would make them happy, but they're actually not happy. But they hang onto it, because they think that it makes them happy. But I don't think they're right. So, like, all the people you're interviewing for this, they're probably not right about their answers to the questions. Like, even me, when you ask me what makes me happy, I probably haven't given you the right answer, because I don't even know if we know.

She felt that many people are unaware of their own happiness and of what makes them happy, which suggests that it is considered a 'truth' that needs to be unveiled or unleashed. That is to say, it is something 'real' about which there exists a 'right idea' and is therefore something that is understood to 'exist' within everyone. The suggestion that people may not have the 'right idea' of what happiness is implies that everyone has *some* idea of happiness, even if it may be 'incorrect'. This therefore indicates that everyone possesses a *capability* of experiencing happiness, even if this blindness to it is also universal.

Nick also expressed that happiness might be something elusive:

> Nick (25, male): Most people don't know what makes them happy, I think. I think most people aren't honest with themselves, the subconscious and denial is a very powerful factor, I think most people use that most of the time.

Like Beth, he also claimed that knowledge of happiness is something that is unknown by the majority of people; however, drawing upon psychological language, he used the ideas of the 'subconscious' and 'denial' to explain this. He also utilised the metaphor of the self being a kind of 'container' for emotion (Lupton, 1998), by suggesting that happiness is something 'real' that is hidden within one's self, but needs to be extracted from the unconscious. Nick also suggested that people might have a better understanding of their own happiness if they were 'honest with themselves'. That is to say that whilst a degree of personal reflection and 'work' on oneself may be required from any individual who wishes to further this understanding, happiness could again be considered to be something that everyone has 'within themselves' but that needs to be unveiled from underneath this 'denial', possibly with the assistance of some kind of psychological 'sophistication' or 'expertise', as Martin suggested:

> Martin (32, male): I guess it takes a certain level of sophistication psychologically to reach a state where you're actually aware of your own happiness. Some people are just very basic and they just eat, sleep, shit, work and that's about it, they probably don't ask themselves many questions.

For Martin, anyone who does not 'ask themselves questions' is 'very basic', and thus less sophisticated, which suggests a desirability of 'knowing oneself' by asking questions. Knowing oneself would provide an individual with an increased awareness of their happiness. Indeed, many self-help texts advocate the idea that it is self-knowledge that 'good selves' ought to strive towards, and that asking oneself questions is a key route to self-improvement (Rimke, 2000). Therefore to situate oneself in this discourse of elusiveness would somewhat allow one to reflect and self-actualise, in order that such an awareness is gained.

Thus, it appears that happiness, like love, is 'knowable only intuitively, at the level of feeling' (Jackson, 1999:100). Indeed, one reason for the dearth of happiness research within sociology may be that happiness is considered to be an elusive emotion, state or process, that which is experienced at the level of the nervous system, which sits outside of the scope of sociological inquiry. However, it is clear here that the idea of happiness being elusive is, in itself, central to the way in which people interpret and articulate it, and it is one of the dominant discourses within which people situate themselves when making sense of what happiness 'is'.

Why is happiness understood by people to be something that needs to be 'unearthed' from the unconscious? Why do people situate themselves within this discourse of elusiveness? This could be because actual feelings and experiences of happiness take place corporeally, at the level of the nervous system (Ekman and Cordaro, 2011) and are thus often difficult to reconcile with the 'outside', material world, despite the fact that happiness is also something inherently social and cultural, both in terms of its construction and the way in which it is experienced.

Despite this commonly held idea that happiness is something elusive and obscured by the unconscious, most people did not appear to find it difficult – when asked – to talk about where they derive their happiness *from*; many of them identified common factors such as friends, family, working life and being in love (factors that have also been highlighted by other social scientists such as Layard (2011) as being important determinants of happiness). Thus, if happiness is something so elusive, how were they able to offer such responses? Very few, if any, claimed psychological 'expertise' in achieving awareness of their happiness; on the other hand, the fact that many of them identified common sources of happiness, such as friends and family, may suggest that attributing happiness to these may simply be dominant discourses that they were replaying. In the same way, describing happiness as something elusive can also be considered another dominant cultural discourse with which it can be made sense of, and it is this idea of elusiveness that is of fundamental importance for the contemporary social construction of happiness. People may indeed know what makes them happy, yet nevertheless make sense of it in this way because of the corporeal, embodied nature of the way in which it is experienced.

'Natural' happiness?

The idea that happiness is something 'natural' – and therefore asocial, like with the discourse of elusiveness – also featured heavily in many people's reflections upon what happiness is. The idea of 'naturalness', which points to the way in which happiness is seen to come from within the body, also parallels a dominant narrative that exists in relation to love, whereby it is commonly understood to be a universal property of human existence (Johnson, 2005). For example, Lizzie (25, female) described the way in which a number of social changes that have taken place over the last few hundred years, such as the rise of consumerism, may have contributed to the way in which *definitions* of happiness might have altered, but that 'the way that you feel inside [...] of happiness [...] that wouldn't have changed. That's just a natural feeling that you get from inside yourself'. An internality is therefore highlighted in relation to happiness here; again, this idea can be related to the metaphor of the body or self as a *container* for happiness, that is, something inside which happiness 'exists' (Lupton, 1998). Further, for Lizzie, as well as for a number of other people, the naturalness of happiness renders it immune or resistant to such wider social change, which is another dominant discourse that has been found to surround definitions of love (Johnson, 2005). The extent to which people feel that happiness might have changed over time or across cultures, and similarities with discourses of love in this respect will be examined further in a later section of this chapter.

A discourse of naturalness was also evident with regard to the way in which interviewees talked about their views on the use in the West today of 'artificial' means of achieving happiness (for instance, anti-depressants and drugs and alcohol). Many expressed negative sentiments towards this, perceiving each of these to be inferior to more 'genuine' experiences of happiness that one should take from 'within oneself', and which are therefore 'natural'. This suggests that there may also be a moral framework underpinning the notion, as drawing happiness from such means is not considered 'right'.

Mark, who had suffered with depression in the past and who had previously taken a course of anti-depressants, felt that such medication is over-prescribed, or 'prescribed willy-nilly':

Mark (41, male): Anti-depressants are prescribed too often. Anti-depressants are for seriological imbalances and stuff like that, if they're going to be given to people with chemical imbalances, that's fine. Anti-depressants that are prescribed willy-nilly, which they frequently are, because my cat's just got run over, and my partner's having an affair, and I've just been made redundant, and I feel miserable [...] oh, here, take these, they'll make you feel better [...] I'm sorry, no. I think they're over-prescribed.

The need to take medication for such seemingly 'mundane' events as the death of one's pet is something that Mark felt was unnecessary. His words could be said to resonate with Nikolas Rose's idea that 'therapeutics has subjectified the mundane' (1996:158). That is, for Rose, everyday life experiences such as debt, marriage, divorce and childbirth have been transformed into emotion-laden 'life events' for which 'coping', 'adjustment' and even medication are required. However, Mark suggested that people who do not have a chemical imbalance, or who are not 'really' depressed ought not to take medication when experiencing such events, thus implying that they should be capable of regaining their happiness 'naturally' rather than 'artificially' (that is, with the assistance of drugs). Others, like Alan, also suggested that emotions are 'natural' aspects of human existence, and therefore attempting to modify emotional experience with 'chemicals' is seemingly undesirable. He felt that to do such a thing is not necessary if one is simply feeling 'a bit fed up', but that instead, 'the condition of human emotion' is something that should exist in and of itself.

> Alan (48, male): I don't think necessarily that the condition of human emotion needs to be medicated for [...] just because you might be getting a bit fed up, doesn't mean to say you should run off to the doctor and say 'excuse me, I'm getting a bit fed up at the moment, can I have a pill to make me not feel fed up?' You know, some happy pills.

Sophie felt that when dealing with adverse events, 'you've got to do things for yourself', rather than rely on any external sources, such as money or other people:

> Sophie (22, female): I think people can rely on these things as well. You know, like how people rely on other drugs, and alcohol. It can become a thing that they can't live without. Which I don't think is very good. But I think people have to learn how to survive without [...] help. Because I think in order to overcome things, you've got to do things for yourself, you've got to say 'this is me, take it or leave it. I'm going to do everything I can to change my life'. Because only you can change your life. People can help you, they could lend you money, or they could give you

advice. But at the end of the day, it's only you that can make a change.

Again, Sophie's claims that 'people have to learn how to survive without help' and that 'only you can change your life' can be linked to the idea that happiness is considered to be something natural, or something that an individual ought to have within him or herself. In other words, happiness for Sophie is not something that one can be *given* by anyone or anything else, but rather one should be able to come to terms with who they are without any kind of aid or assistance (by saying 'this is me, take it or leave it'). In this account, Sophie situates herself not only within a discourse of naturalness, but also within a therapeutic discourse. Taking responsibility for one's own happiness in this way, and engaging in techniques in order to improve one's life are intimately bound up with the concept of 'working' on the self, 'caring' for the self (Foucault, 1988) and with therapeutic discourse, which these concepts are aspects of. Self-sufficiency in this way is also something that is championed by self-help literature, whereby the importance of both relying on oneself throughout one's life, as well as 'forming a healthy relationship with the self' (Hazleden, 2003:421) is emphasised. Indeed, Sophie's account echoes advice offered to self-help author Melody Beattie's readers: 'Self-care is an attitude toward ourselves and our lives that says, I am responsible for myself [...]I am responsible for how much I enjoy life, for how much pleasure I find in daily activities [...] My decisions will take into account my responsibilities to myself' (Beattie, 1992:114).

Thus, making sense of happiness through a discourse of naturalness gives rise to the idea that it is one's own personal responsibility to change their life and to find a solution to problems, and that dependency on sources external to oneself is undesirable. This can be associated with the 'enterprise culture' of neoliberal societies, wherein individuals who are able to care for and take responsibility for themselves are well-placed to be 'effective' citizens who are then able to govern themselves (Rose, 1996, Rimke, 2000; see Chapter 2 for further discussion). In this case, then, if one were to gain happiness from an external source, taking responsibility for maintaining it thereafter would be more problematic than if they had found it 'within themselves'.

Biological happiness

Related both to the idea that happiness is natural as well as to its embodied nature (as discussed in the section on elusiveness) is the way in which some respondents situated themselves within a biological discourse of happiness, that is, attributing it to biological or chemical processes such as the release of endorphins or serotonin. As with the discourses of naturalness and elusiveness, a biological discourse has also been shown to be a dominant discourse within which people situate themselves in relation to their perceptions of love. In this case, love is also made sense of as a chemical reaction to another person (Johnson, 2005).

Mark described happiness as 'a chemical', and Martin commented on how he feels when exposed to sunlight and attributed this to vitamin intake:

> LH: *What do you think happiness is?*
>
> Mark (41, male) : [long pause] I think physiologically it's a chemical […] erm […] it's serotonin, isn't it[. . .]
>
> Martin (32, male): […]happiness is a physical sensation as well. Like, two weeks ago when the sun was out for once in a while, I sat on my balcony for four hours and after that, I felt so good. 'Cos for the first time in half a year I got Vitamin D in me. […] I tend to have a biological opinion of what makes you happy.

This suggests that for both Mark and Martin, as long as an individual had some intake of Vitamin D or release of serotonin, the idea that happiness 'is a physical sensation' means that they could experience happiness irrespective of any social circumstances that they may be in, and also suggests that happiness is natural, or something that is derived from within the individual. Again, then, the idea that the body is a container for one's happiness (Lupton, 1998) is utilised here. At another point in the interview, Martin also explained that he had previously suffered from seasonal affective disorder (SAD), with which he experienced feelings of depression in winter months when exposed to fewer hours of sunlight. This is also a common discourse drawn upon in contemporary society, particularly as we witness an increasing popularity of the use of 'light boxes', which people use to simulate sunlight in order to combat feelings of depression that they feel are brought about by prolonged periods of darkness. The idea that we should feel happier when exposed to more sunlight (which a number of respondents emphasised) is linked to scientific evidence that exposure to bright light increases levels of the neurotransmitter serotonin in the brain (Leppamaki et al., 2002, Lumie, 2014), and it is evidence of this nature which has been produced by scientific professionals, that is drawn upon here.

Whilst people make sense of and describe happiness as innate and individually and internally felt, it could also be said that these corporeal feelings are socially ordered and are given some kind of cultural meaning and significance, and are thus drawn upon in the form of a discourse with which to make sense of them.

Such a biological discourse of happiness appears to run counter to that of naturalness explored above. One could ask: is reliance upon sunlight and vitamin intake for one's happiness not comparable to relying upon other 'external' sources such as drugs, alcohol or therapists? Whilst negative sentiments were expressed, as has been seen, by many respondents towards the use of these, they did not seem to express the same negativity towards requiring sunlight and vitamins for experiences of happiness. On the other hand, conceiving of happiness as a 'physical sensation' does indeed relate to the idea that it is something natural and internal to one's self, and the idea that we ought to take responsibility for our own happiness could still apply here; whilst it would be harder to take responsibility for one's emotional state if the weather were bad, as this is something that we as individuals have no control over, 'solutions' to this, such as the purchase of a 'light box', or taking holidays to destinations with more sun exposure were highlighted as potential ways in which to do so. Thus, positioning oneself in biological discourse would still allow people to be proactive in attempting to manage their happiness. It seems that here then people are drawing upon scientific knowledge related to serotonin and vitamin intake in order to then situate themselves within this biological discourse of happiness, and that the fact that such information has been properly 'evidenced' by qualified 'experts' (scientists) such as Leppamaki et al. (2002) may give it heightened cultural and social importance and credibility.

Thus, in reflecting upon the idea of happiness through a framework of biological discourse, one would acknowledge happiness as a feeling that pre-exists the selves that experience it; it is something brought about by chemical and biological processes. However, it is important to bear in mind here that in understanding happiness through discourse as sociologists, happiness itself is produced *through* the language and discourse that are used in making sense of it.

Unique feelings

Another common idea expressed by a number of people is that happiness is something individual and unique. In other words, happiness was seen to be something that each individual would experience differently, that it is manifested through one's personality and plays a key role in the way in which one constructs and reconstructs their personal identity. What is interesting here is that whilst many interviewees asserted such a view, their accounts of and reflections upon happiness – unbeknownst to them – shared many similarities. Indeed, this book rests on the very premise that Westerners (and British people) make sense of happiness in culturally rooted and socially patterned ways and documents the ways in which this is done. It is ironic, then, that this particular way in which happiness is commonly made sense of stands in direct contradiction to a sociological understanding of happiness! Alan, for example, described the way in which his 'version' of happiness is probably unique and different to anyone else's:

> Alan (48, male): I would imagine it's radically different in some cases, I would think there'd be a broad spectrum, I wouldn't necessarily say my version of happiness is [...] replicable [...] or applicable to other people.

He suggested that there is a 'broad spectrum' of different variations of happiness, on which his version would feature. People may situate themselves within such a discourse because happiness is something that is experienced or felt at the level of the nervous system and is therefore perceived to stem from one's unconscious (as is discussed previously, in relation to the elusiveness of happiness). It may also be for this reason that happiness is considered to be something 'natural' and 'internally' felt and conceived of by drawing upon a biological discourse.

Some respondents also felt that to be happy is 'a personality thing', that is, something that one is born with (which again, links closely with the discourse of naturalness already discussed). Indeed, some even used the word 'natural' to describe this, like Linda:

> Linda (65, female): I think some people are naturally happier personalities than others[...]

Linda's comment suggests that she too sees happiness as something natural and therefore immune or resistant to any social or circumstantial change. Beth also expressed this view:

> Beth (23, female): I think some people are just generally happy, aren't they [...] just all the time. Yeah, I think it's a personality thing. I don't think it's your situation at all, I think it's your personality, as a person. Like, some people are always [...] not happy, even if they're in a picture-perfect life.

Thus, for Beth, happiness is something that is out of one's control and cannot be affected by situational factors; the idea that it is 'a personality thing' again suggests that happiness is something natural.

People also expressed the idea that to be happy is part of one's identity. Whilst this idea is similar to that of happiness as one's personality, identity – rather than being considered as something fixed and natural – is something that can be constructed and reconstructed throughout one's life, and it is this process of construction that is where happiness, for many, can be gained. For example, Nick described happiness as 'moving forward':

> Nick (25, male): I think happiness is [...] [pauses] moving forward. Happiness is moving forward, and indulging your true self.
> *LH: What do you mean by indulging your true self?*
> Nick (25, male): Being brave enough to admit that this is what you really want. And then facing the consequences if that doesn't happen. [...] I think that's what happiness is. Working out your needs, and trying to achieve them, not necessarily achieving them.

By describing being happy as the indulgence of one's 'true self', Nick suggests that happiness is intimately linked with being able to understand and come to terms with one's identity or self, by 'working out your needs', thus attempting to reconstruct it as necessary (rather than accepting it as something fixed and unchangeable, like personality). This appears contradictory to happiness as an aspect of personality, as here it is understood that one can 'work on' and further understand their identity, which is thus very much within their control. It seems then, that people undertake a process of negotiation between the way in which their personality determines or even constrains their experiences of happiness, as well as the way in which the self can be modified in order that happiness is maximised.

Thus, considering happiness as an aspect of one's personality and identity suggests that it is something longer-term and part of the self throughout an individual's life, as well as having a shorter-term, momentary nature (which will be explored in a later section). Both of these demonstrate that people are also situating themselves in a discourse of the uniqueness and individuality of happiness. This resonates with elements of therapeutic discourse (Furedi, 2004, Illouz, 2007, Rieff, 1966, Rose, 1996) in which contemporary individuals position themselves within a narrative in which they are able to 'work' on themselves and their identities in order to self-actualise and further their well-being. This will be explored in more detail in the following chapter of the book.

'It's almost one's duty to be happy': Happiness and positive thinking

Strong emphasis was placed by many people upon the importance of positive thinking for a happy life. Such a narrative originates from self-help literature and culture and has subsequently pervaded other realms of cultural and social life (Ehrenreich, 2010). Not only has self-help culture permeated the wider market, leading to the proliferation of a 'happiness industry' in which the idea of 'happiness' has been attached to a range of marketable products and services, such as books and classes, but its elements can also be found in popular culture and the media, in which we have witnessed a growing popularity of programmes and advertisements centred around the enhancement of lifestyles. It is also evident in schools and universities where students are encouraged to attend sessions and classes on maintaining a positive attitude to their studies and to life in general (Ecclestone and Hayes, 2009).

A widespread view found amongst many was that happiness is something that should be universally and actively striven for in life, even when suffering may stand as an obstacle to this. Alan described happiness as 'one's duty':

> Alan (48, male): [...] it's almost one's duty to be happy. You know, it's easy to be unhappy and happiness can take an effort. You can look at the bright side, you know. Is it half empty or half full [...] well I can look at it as half full, and therefore it is an attitude.

Alan distinguishes between 'half empty' and 'half full' attitudes towards life and said you should 'look at the bright side'; this suggests that we have *choice* over the approach that we take to the way we live (that is, between whether we see the glass as half empty or full, or whether or not we have a positive attitude), being thus in keeping with theories that advocate the idea that we as individuals strive for personal fulfilment via acts of choice in neoliberal democracies (Rose, 1996: see Chapter 2 for further discussion).

Despite happiness being considered a 'duty', for Alan, it is also something that requires *effort*, or putting it another way, something that needs to be 'worked on', in order for this duty to be fulfilled. The idea that we ought to work on our happiness stems from this discourse of positive thinking that is advocated by the self-help industry.

Similarly, Beth said that 'you've just got to force yourself' to be happy, even during unhappy periods and Chloe recalled how she felt at the time of a recent relationship break-up:

> Chloe (26, female): I take control of my own happiness [...] like, it's very rare that I would let myself get that down. [...] when I broke up with [ex-boyfriend], I was like, actually I am going to be fine with this. And I'm gonna be more fine if I think myself there.

She particularly stressed that 'thinking herself' to be fine, or thinking positive thoughts would result in the maintenance of some degree of happiness in such an adverse circumstance, which echoes one of the fundamental precepts of the positive thinking discourse found in self-help literature (such as that found in popular texts like *Feel the Fear and Do It Anyway* (Jeffers, 1997), which emphasises positive thinking as a way of reducing fear). Thinking, then, is a technology or a technique that one can employ in order to transform oneself into a happier or more positive person. This is also a central feature of therapeutic discourse (Furedi, 2004, Illouz, 2007, Rose, 1996), which will be explored further in the following chapter. To not 'let oneself get that down' and to 'take control' of one's happiness also tie in with this precept. Both sit at the intersection of positive thinking on one hand, and social control on the other; the cultural importance of displaying a relatively happy attitude to life, which is widely acknowledged in the Western world, ensures that one would 'work' to keep their happiness level at a certain point and to prevent it from falling below a particular threshold which would be viewed by society as undesirable. Indeed, it can be seen from these quotes that unhappiness is regarded as a feeling that needs to ultimately be managed, so that it is reduced or eradicated. One would also engage in practises that would help them to 'take control' of their happiness and to thus take responsibility for it, which would again, require a need for it to be 'worked' on. Such practises, as discussed in Chapter 2, are bound up with the political programmes of neoliberal democracies, wherein people who are happy in this way would have the ability to be 'effective' citizens who take care of themselves and of their happiness or unhappiness (Hazleden, 2003, Rimke, 2000, Rose, 1996).

Tom made a more implicit acknowledgement of the importance of positive thinking and the idea of happiness being a 'duty', by admitting that to say he felt *un*happy brought about a feeling of guilt, as 'there's always someone worse off that you':

> Tom (25, male): I don't know, I've got this kind of guilt about saying that I'm not happy, I think it's like I'm feeling sorry for myself, I'm just dwelling on things.
>
> *LH: Why do you feel guilty about saying that you're not happy?*
>
> Tom (25, male): Well, you know, there's always someone else worse off than you. And, I'm unhappy with what's going on in my life at the moment, but I've got my family, I've got good friends, you know there's people who are worse off than me [...] I don't know, maybe it's a bit self-indulgent to say I'm unhappy, when there's a lot worse things that could be happening to me at the moment.

Tom may have felt guilty about admitting to feeling unhappy because making such an admission runs counter to the positive thinking discourse of happiness that many individuals appear to situate themselves in. If this discourse is so widely drawn upon, then any display of discontent or misery may be considered as socially undesirable. Furthermore, whilst Tom himself acknowledged this undesirability – by describing himself as 'self-indulgent' as well as stating that 'there's a lot worse things that could be happening to me' – his feeling of guilt is also an indication that other members of society may disapprove of his unhappiness. This again then, is an illustration of the way in which such a positive thinking discourse acts to facilitate social control; the failure to display a positive attitude to life may elicit a feeling of guilt, which – as symbolic interactionist Shott (1979) writes – is a 'role-taking emotion', or one that involves 'putting oneself in another's position and taking that person's perspective' (1979:1323). Guilt, Shott writes, is one of a number of emotions that involves an individual reflecting on how they come across to others and may be elicited if he or she realises that others might view their self-presentation as negative or 'undesirable', thus providing motivation for more normative conduct (which, in this case, would be a display of happiness or contentment). Therefore, Tom's feeling of guilt led him to reflect upon and identify the *positive* aspects of his life (that is, good friends and family), in order to attempt to put on such a display.

As shall be seen in the following section, many interviewees also highlighted the inevitability and 'normal' nature of sad or negative experiences. On first glance, this could be said to be contradictory to such a positive thinking discourse; surely people should seek to *avoid* or *prevent* adverse events and unhappy experiences? However, by saying that such occasions are beneficial for the enhancement of *positive* experiences, it can be seen that these are actually considered to be a contribution to positive thinking, as Ehrenreich (2010) found in her study of the experiences of breast cancer sufferers in terms of the positive outcomes and effects that they accorded to this.

So, as can be seen, situating oneself within a discourse of positive thinking allows individuals the capacity and ability to 'work' on their happiness and ensure that potential for positive experiences is maximised. Such a discourse also acts to facilitate a kind of emotional control; as long as people constantly undertake this 'work', they will constantly be aiming to ensure that their happiness remains at a level deemed desirable by society. Any failure to conform to positive thinking (that is, experiencing and displaying unhappiness, and therefore contradicting the tenets of the discourse) may also elicit 'negative' emotions such as guilt or shame (Shott, 1979), thus motivating individuals to attempt to regain a more normative (or 'happy') emotional display.

'It's not normal to be happy all the time': The transience of happiness

An idea frequently reflected on by those interviewed was the idea that happiness is something transient, or – in the words of Mark (41, male) – something that 'can be snatched away'. Many acknowledged that there is a need to achieve *balance* between happy and more negative experiences. A duality was also identified, as respondents distinguished this shorter-term, variable happiness as something different from one which is longer-term, which many made sense of in relation to the evaluation of their lives overall and as an element of their identities and selfhood (and like that which was explored in the previous section).

A number of people talked about the way in which negative or unpleasant experiences are an inevitable part of life, and therefore one cannot and should not expect to be happy at all times. As Gillian said, to always be happy is 'not normal':

> Gillian (45, female): I think to get depressed now and again is quite natural. There's always gonna be death, there's always gonna be break-ups, there's always going to be, you know, something's fallen through that you can't have [...] you know, there's always going to be disappointment and there's always going to be sad times. Especially with bereavement. And that is part of life. Like what I said at the beginning, it's not normal to be happy all the time.

In outlining the transient nature of happiness, Gillian does so through drawing upon the naturalness discourse and expressed that occasionally felt negative feelings, or feelings of depression are also 'natural', and that such emotions and the experience of adverse life events are a universal inevitability of life. The idea that 'it's not normal to be happy all the time', also suggests that that there is a 'natural' dimension to the way that happiness is experienced, as well as a framework of norms. That is to say, whilst it might be deemed as socially 'undesirable' to be persistently depressed (as this would run counter to the positive thinking discourse explored in the previous section), positioning oneself within this discourse of 'transience' would also suggest an undesirability of persistent *happiness*. Indeed, Chris expressed this view after being asked the question 'Who is the happiest person you know?':

> Chris (46, male): I guess I have a sort of mistrust of other people who are consistently happy, because I've met people who have seemed very happy but have then thrown themselves off a bridge. So to me, it's like, you can demonstrate it, but that's not necessarily who you really are. You know, I'm a little wary of it. I mean, I think the happiest person is probably the village idiot! Isn't that awful, that I view permanent happiness as being a mental dysfunction? [laughs]

Thus, Chris' assertion that an individual experiencing permanent happiness would have to be the 'village idiot' and would be likely to have a 'mental dysfunction' illustrates the idea that this would not only be abnormal, but also socially undesirable. Anyone who does display constant happiness is unlikely to be giving a genuine 'performance' and may not be expressing his or her 'true' identity (as such a display is 'not necessarily who you really are'). Chris then, not only identifies happiness as transient, but also draws upon both the biological discourse (through associating happiness with mental functioning) and the discourse of uniqueness and individuality (through distinguishing displays of happiness from happy identities or personalities). In addition to this, happiness for Chris can also be a part of a 'performance', in which it may be displayed regardless of whether or not one 'feels' happy (akin to the work of Goffman, 1959 and Hochschild, 1979). Although we are constantly needing to 'manage' our emotions in accordance with culturally specific 'feeling rules' in situations that prescribe this (such as the workplace – see Hochschild, 1979, 1983), happiness that is 'managed' unsuccessfully may be perceived negatively by others if the individual doing so is unable to convince others that he or she is happy. A permanent display of happiness may, furthermore, be likely to be regarded by others as 'false' or 'artificial'.

A large number of respondents emphasised a need to recognise the benefits of periodic feelings of unhappiness or misery, in order that happy times can be recognised and fully appreciated. In other words, *balance* between the two was not only accorded with a social 'desirability' (as it is 'quite natural' to experience negative emotion) but also to have importance for people's well-being. Laurence, for example, described constant happiness as 'stifling' and compared it to living in 'cuckoo land':

> LH: *Do you think that to be happy all the time would be a good thing?*
> Laurence (65, male): No. To be happy all the time would be so [...] stifling. You know, I mean, you'd be living in cuckoo land, it just wouldn't be real. I think we've got to be unhappy at times, to make us realise just how fortunate we really are. But being happy all the time, it just wouldn't work.

Thus, like Chris, Laurence expressed a social undesirability towards permanent happiness, by saying that that one who experienced this would not be giving a 'real' performance. Thus, a display of happiness that is 'managed' would, again, also be regarded in a negative light if the 'actor' was unable to convince his or her 'audience' of its genuineness (Goffman, 1959). For both Chris and Laurence, a display of permanent happiness would almost certainly not be 'real', due to the normative expectation that people cannot be happy all of the time. This would also be detrimental to the individual's well-being, as it would be 'stifling'; Laurence highlighted the way in which negative events can enhance positive ones, as they serve as confirmation for the individual of the aspects of life that they *can* feel good about. Tom also expressed the view that negative events are a conduit to positive ones and felt that 'taking the rough with the smooth' was important in terms of giving an individual motivation to 'come forward and progress', or in other words, the provision of a capacity for *self-fulfilment* and *self-actualisation*:

> Tom (25, male): I think you've got to take the rough with the smooth. You know, life isn't one constant up. You know, you go

up and down, up and down, that's life. You know, you might get yourself a great job and earn good money, you might get to lots of good gigs, or Arsenal winning in the league, I don't know, but then the next week you might get dumped by your girlfriend. And then you feel crap! So you can't always be happy. I think it's important to feel that sense of crap [...] unhappiness, to make you want to come forward and progress. That's what I think is important.

Thus, it could be argued that for the autonomous, free individual living in advanced liberal democracies that is highlighted by Rose (1996), a requisite amount of experienced misery is a necessary ingredient for enabling the maximisation of one's potential and fulfilment.

Now, it might appear here that this transience discourse that many people are situating themselves in stands in contradiction to the positive thinking discourse explored in the previous section. Surely if the positive thinking discourse advocates a positive attitude towards life and discourages the expression of any negative emotions, then should it not be considered 'normal' or 'natural' to feel these? However, by examining the way in which the respondents have talked about these emotions or experiences, the fact that they talk about them as conduits to positive experience and happiness shows that they do indeed subscribe to this way of thinking; despite acknowledging the importance of adversity and misery, they also in turn acknowledge their fundamental and positive role in the enhancement of happiness at other points in time.

The idea that happiness is transient, then, appears to also be directly opposed to that which was raised in a previous section concerning the way in which happiness is considered to be an aspect of a person's *identity* or *personality*. As well as highlighting the short-term, transitory and often emotional nature of happiness, many respondents reasoned that this is in fact one of two types of happiness, the second being something longer term, pertaining to life as a whole, and identity and selfhood. Nick described how, for him, happiness can 'exist on two different levels':

LH: *Do you think that happiness is a short-term, fleeting feeling, or is it longer-lasting?*

> Nick (25, male): I think there are various levels, because [...] I think happiness in a way is like a drug. It's like, you can get different types of highs, you know, so [...] you could get, like a 'I've got a job' high, which is like [makes a sudden gasping sound], or you could get [...] like now, I feel quite [...] good about my life. [...] So you can have a general contentment, I think it can exist on two different levels.

He described happiness as being 'like a drug', in terms of the 'different types of highs' that one can experience, be it something fleeting, sudden and intense, or something more constant with a lower intensity.

Thus to situate oneself in the discourse of transience is to conceive of this particular 'type' of happiness as something fleeting and non-permanent, and this therefore suggests that misery is seen as an inevitable part of human experience. Furthermore, misery is constructed in this way, and via the positive thinking discourse, as a beneficial conduit to happiness and self-fulfilment. The transience discourse is also partnered with the *naturalness* discourse discussed previously, as the experience of misery and sadness is described as 'natural' or 'normal'. So, whilst positive thinking discourse advocates that too much *un*happiness is socially undesirable, the transience discourse advocates that too much *happiness* is 'unnatural'. Thus positioning oneself in each of these discourses of happiness means that a personal *compromise* needs to be reached in order that a requisite amount of happiness can be expressed and experienced.

Happiness across time and space: Evolving or unchanging?

Has the idea of happiness changed or evolved over time and history? Does it differ across cultures? These questions were asked of interviewees in order to be able to gather a better understanding of what they think happiness *is* in the contemporary Western world, as compared to other cultures and at other time-points. In terms of time, many of them identified a number of social changes and processes that have taken place in contemporary Western society, such as increased consumerism and a growing emphasis on the importance of body image, that have impacted upon what might *make* us happy.

The rise of consumerism in the West was identified by many as a major factor in the way in which the idea of happiness might vary across time and space, both in terms of the way in which it is defined and experienced. Many respondents talked about the way in which members of society have become increasingly preoccupied with the accumulation of money and the consumption of material goods, as well as the idea that wealth and material possessions have become a main source of happiness for many in society; many respondents expressed this view, despite also – at other points during their interviews – expressing the widespread sentiment that the accumulation of money, for them personally, cannot yield happiness. Gillian, for example, talked about the negative impact of consumption, whilst emphasising the way in which some – particularly young people – might derive a perceived but 'false' sense of happiness from it:

> Gillian (45, female): I actually think that young people think they're happier 'cos they've got all the material things, but they're actually unhappier because of the pressures and responsibilities that they now have. Even paying their mobile phone bill, that was something that would never have crossed my mind when I was a kid, you know? You didn't have a mobile phone [...] now, it's more image conscious, you know, what brand you're wearing [...] I think that makes a lot of kids unhappy. Especially if they can't afford the big brands and they don't want to, you know, be seen in a cheap pair of trainers, and stuff like that. It's all nonsense, really. But that's the way that things are being portrayed.

Increased consumerism, emphasis on body image and appearance and 'celebrity culture' are considered to have replaced religion as sources of happiness as society has progressed. Chris felt that whilst a belief in God and the church once stood at the basis of one's set of guiding principles in life, this has now been 'replaced by this kind of competition in terms of how you look', which has become an integral part of an increasingly individualistic society:

> Chris (46, male): I think the rise of [...] especially in the West, the rise of the concept of the individual, it becomes very much what the individual views as being happiness, whereas I think

happiness was much more of a collective thing at one point, I mean we had [...] there was almost a jingoistic patriotism, so you were happy to see your country win a war.

Whilst Chris identified individualisation as a social change that has impacted upon 'what the individual views as being happiness', he does so through acknowledging the uniqueness and individuality discourse discussed previously, by explaining that happiness is now something that is seen to be experienced on an *individual* level, rather than as a collective.

A breakdown of normative frameworks was also associated with the changing nature of happiness; this was expressed particularly by Eileen (63, female), Helen (77, female) and Maureen (80, female), three of the oldest respondents. Each of them identified an erosion of values and morals – which they felt was partly due to the decline of religion and changes in the law – as a means by which society might be becoming less happy. Helen expressed a 'fantasy' about the past:

LH: *Do you think that the idea of happiness might have changed over time, or over history?*

Helen (77, female): Yes, it has. Because the world is now a different place [...] the youth of today make it [...] not so easy for children to play outside during the day. You don't know who's walking around [...] it's not like it used to be, it's different. This country has changed beyond all recognition. And the children, because of the laws of this country now about disciplining children, that you're not allowed to slap them and you're not allowed to do this or that, consequently, they're very rude to their parents [...] [...] If their children are good children, and don't give them any worries or problems, then their happiness is derived from that. It's when their children start mixing with the wrong sort of people, because once they go out of the house, it's the influence outside that determines the way they go in life. Well that's my opinion.

As society becomes increasingly characterised by discourses of individuality, uniqueness and naturalness (as has been explored above), an illusory image of a normless society may emerge for many people. Older people like Helen – in describing how this is taking place – may thus express nostalgia in doing so for past times in which normative frameworks might have been more concrete and tangible.

Lizzie, whilst acknowledging social changes and processes that are likely to have impacted on the lives of contemporary Westerners like many of the other respondents, identified a 'true', 'inner' and more 'natural' happiness experienced by the individual that is more resistant to such change:

> Lizzie (25, female): For people to be happy, say four or five hundred years ago, they would be in a relationship quite quickly, producing children quite quickly [...] whereas these days, happiness is usually derived either from [...] often consumerism, people often feel happy that I know, who have got brand new clothes, a fast car, a nice house, and that has an impact [...] on their life. [...] But say [...] overall your goals, the way that you feel inside [...] of happiness [...] that wouldn't have changed. That's just a natural feeling that you get from inside yourself.

Lizzie makes the assumption that happiness *existed* and was *recognised* several hundred years ago and draws upon a discourse of marriage and family – concerned with being in a relationship and having children – that has been dominant in modern societies, whereby choosing to enter into such a unit is likely to lead to happiness. She felt that what *makes* us happy may have changed over time, but the fact that happiness is something natural and internal means that its essence has remained the same – that is, that it is a trans-historical part of life.

Thus, increased consumerism, a wider variety of lifestyle choices and a breakdown of normative frameworks are all factors that have been identified as contributors to the changing nature of happiness in contemporary society; many have suggested that some of these have led to a *decline* in happiness levels. However, the idea that a 'natural', 'inner' happiness exists, which is supposedly trans-historical and thus immune and resistant to these wider social changes means that the variability of happiness which was talked about by many respondents may in fact simply affect the way in which happiness is *reflected* upon (for example, in terms of what might *make* people happy), whilst subjective *experience* of it could be said to have remained the same. Thus, in reflecting upon the changing nature of happiness across time and space, people appear to situate themselves within the discourse of *naturalness*, as they have disconnected the idea of a 'natural', innate happiness from wider social and cultural changes that have taken place over time. This – as with many of the other dominant discourses of happiness explored in this chapter – echoes that which has also been argued about love; that is, 'even when placed within elaborate and sophisticated understandings of the changing patterns of heterosexual relationships, the ideal of love is reified as an absolute given because it is "natural"' (Johnson, 2005:44). Despite acknowledgement of wider social changes that may have changed ideas surrounding what makes people happy, happiness too, is reified through this discourse, as something that is tangible, real and existing within the body. Because of these properties, the 'feeling' of happiness is said to have remained the same. This therefore suggests that happiness is understood as something *asocial*, or something that can be experienced 'outside' of society. Therefore this, as well as the way in which people drew upon the biological and elusiveness discourses, in which happiness was conceived as something bodily, or cerebral, suggests that it is not seen as something necessarily social but as part of human nature, despite social changes that have taken place that have made some contribution to the way in which happiness has been socially constructed. It is this naturalness discourse that seems to be more widely drawn-upon – and happiness, whilst social factors are acknowledged (as can be seen above), in this way is seen to transcend any social and cultural frameworks that exist alongside it.

Conclusion

When reflecting upon the idea of happiness and making sense of one's experiences of it, people situate themselves within a number of dominant discourses, which together paint a picture of what they think happiness is and illustrate the way in which happiness is a complex social construction. It has also shed light on the way in which discourse is used in the production of accounts of happiness and can now be used as an intricate backdrop against which we can begin to understand the happiness of Westerners and, more specifically, British people.

It is through the positive thinking discourse – in which happiness is considered to be 'almost one's duty' – that to be persistently *un*happy is considered socially 'undesirable'; however, this must be carefully negotiated in relation to tenets of the transience discourse, as this specifies that it would also be 'unnatural' and 'inauthentic' to experience or display continual *happiness*. Thus, in terms of each of these discourses, an individual must adhere to the framework of norms that pertain to 'appropriate' levels of expression and display of happiness. People also situate themselves within a uniqueness and individuality discourse; here, happiness is considered to be experienced in a unique way by every individual and is regarded as a key aspect of both identity (which can be 'worked on' and reconstructed) and personality (which is relatively fixed and 'natural'). In drawing upon the discourses of naturalness, elusiveness and biology, happiness is conceived of as something natural, produced 'within' oneself, whether corporeally or from within the unconscious. It is also in this way that the naturalness of happiness is maintained across time and space, so whilst social factors are acknowledged by many (as can be seen in this chapter) as having the power to change the *causes* of happiness over time and space, the 'feeling' itself is seen to transcend any social and cultural frameworks that exist alongside it. All of this illustrates the way in which happiness is a complex social construction; by showing how we situate ourselves in each of these dominant discourses, it can be seen that on the one hand, happiness is characterised by essentiality, rendering it immune and resistant to social factors, whilst simultaneously being located within a complex normative framework in which exists cultural guidelines on the way in which happiness ought to be displayed and experienced.

4
The Happy Self: Understanding Happiness through Therapeutic Discourse

In a further attempt to construct a sociocultural backdrop against which happiness can be understood, this chapter examines the way in which people situate themselves within therapeutic discourse when reflecting upon the idea of happiness. Whilst the discourses explored in the previous chapter were concerned with what happiness is considered to *be*, this is one that frames people's *experiences* and *conceptions* of happiness. An understanding of the relationship between happiness and therapeutic discourse is again fundamental to obtaining an insight into the way in which happiness is socially constructed in Britain and parts of the contemporary Western world, and it can help to illustrate the ways in which people use discourse more generally in producing accounts of their experiences and perceptions of happiness.

Therapeutic discourse is a facet of the therapeutic 'turn' that modern Western societies have been said to be increasingly characterised by over the last 50 or so years. This is discussed in detail in Chapter 2 of this book, and I shall thus only outline this briefly here.

Frank Furedi (2004) talks about the way in which 'therapeutic language and practices have expanded into everyday life' (2004:1). He argues that everyday experiences and activities are being talked and thought about in a more 'emotional' way, and that words which were previously confined to the realm of psychotherapy and psychology (or the 'psy sciences'), such as 'stress', 'anxiety', 'trauma' and 'syndrome' are now commonly appearing in our everyday vocabulary to describe not just troublesome experiences, but also those considered 'normal'; everyday life experiences such as debt, marriage, divorce and childbirth have been transformed into emotion-laden 'life events' for which 'coping' and 'adjustment' are required. Such a discourse, which many argue is quintessentially modern and a defining feature of modern societies, is also characterised by a distinct individualism whereby the needs of the individual and the self are of paramount importance, rather than that of the community, society or common good, and self-sufficiency and self-knowledge are encouraged. Much of this originates directly from the therapy industry and self-help literature.

Many sociologists, such as Rieff (1966), Lasch (1979) and Furedi (2004) have considered the therapeutic turn and the increasing individualisation of modern societies as a movement towards the decline or breakdown of culture, values and community as such practices have permeated numerous realms of social life. Others, on the other hand, acknowledge it more positively as something that has enabled a space to emerge in the public domain for legitimate discussion of personal pain and emotion (Wright, 2008). Whichever of these is the case, I, in this chapter, aim to simply explain and chart the way in which therapeutic discourse and such psychological and emotional language has been drawn upon by interviewees to produce accounts of their experiences of happiness (and indeed, unhappiness).

For many people, the experience of happiness was found to be closely related to therapeutic precepts that are concerned with the self: in particular, self-care and self-knowledge, which are both qualities or values that are strongly advocated by the therapy industry and self-help literature (Rimke, 2000). Factors such as being in control of life, the feeling of being accepted by others, the possession of a certain degree of self-confidence and awareness of one's needs and personal aspirations were all considered to be fundamental for a happy life. Inability or failure to achieve these would, for them, result in unhappiness. Thus, for those who situate themselves within therapeutic discourse, to be happy is to conform to such precepts; many respondents did so despite never having been consumers of the therapy industry.

Thus, this chapter will firstly demonstrate the way in which people made sense of happiness as something that is to be both sought and achieved by the *individual*, with minimal input from other people or factors; it will then go on to look at the way in which people acknowledged a need for 'work' on and control over one's self in order to be happy. Next, it will show how some interviewees described *un*happy experiences in a very introspective way, whereby psychological language was used in describing a range of life events, before going on to examine the way in which some people reflected upon the interview experience itself using therapeutic language. Intersections between this and the discourses discussed in the previous chapter will be highlighted when applicable, particularly those of elusiveness, naturalness, biological, uniqueness and positive thinking. However, before undertaking an examination of this, I will firstly consider the views and opinions of the respondents towards the therapy industry itself.

Views on the therapy industry

All respondents were asked for their views on the therapy industry, particularly psychotherapy and counselling, as well as psychiatric medication like anti-depressants. Despite the fact that many of them – as will be shown below – positioned themselves in therapeutic discourse and made sense of happiness via 'psy' ideas, many also claimed to be sceptical about the therapy industry itself. Each of the three accounts below demonstrate a degree of disapproval towards it. What is particularly interesting about the accounts of Tom, Chris and Beth, which are presented here, is that they all distinguish between cases where therapy or medication for an individual may be necessary or acceptable (which they felt were a small minority of individuals), and others where it is not; it is this latter category which they all highlighted as a growing 'problem' in society:

> LH: *Some people take anti-depressants or see therapists and counsellors in order to feel happy or happier these days. What do you think about this?*
> Tom (25, male): I think some people genuinely need that bit of help. But I also think a lot of people think that it's the done thing to do, and that it's the easy option. I mean, there's history of mental illness in my family, so I've known people who have been genuinely ill, they've needed counselling, or therapy, or drugs or whatever. I've always compared myself to them and said, you know, I'm better off than them because I don't feel I need it. And I think it's culture as well, like, my family are

northern, their attitude is 'don't be soft', you know, just get on with it. I guess that's a different attitude to some families in the south...you know you hear about these kids who have been prescribed anti-depressants when they're about seven or eight years old....I don't know, personally I think...You can numb the issues, you can numb the pain, but if you're depressed about something, say, about being single, you can take anti-depressants, but if you're still single, you're only suppressing it. You know, maybe people should just try and accept it, or do something about it.

Tom distinguished between people who are 'genuinely ill' and who may need therapeutic intervention, and others who are not, and who simply see it to be the 'done thing to do', and attributed the latter attitude to those living in the south of the country; he identified a difference in opinion between those living in the south and the north. Tom's words could be interpreted as resonating with the naturalness discourse highlighted in the preceding chapter; in using the example of singleness as a hypothetical reason for an individual's feeling of unhappiness, he suggests that one should simply 'do something about it' rather than rely on therapy or drugs to suppress the feeling. This implies that the latter may simply provide an 'unnatural' shield from unhappiness that is nevertheless unable to eradicate it.

Chris also emphasised, like Tom, that to seek therapy or medication if one is 'in crisis' or has an emotional or mental 'scar' is acceptable:

Chris (46, male): I think if people are in crisis, or having depression, if medication is needed, or if therapy is needed because of a scar, then I think that's very valid. But Freudians used to say that you had to have eight years of constant analysis before you can even start to be cured. Well I don't agree with that, I think that builds a dependency, between the therapist and patient. But on top of that, I think there are certain aspects of your personality that you're never going to cure. You know, they're just part of who you are. It's like, I knew someone who was a depressive and he said 'why is it that everybody goes "you're dealing with your depression"? Why don't they just say "you're living with your depression"?'. Like, it becomes this disease...well maybe it's not a disease, maybe it's just...a way of being. And does it really need to be cured? I know people who've...because of the circumstances their life's built up, they get to a crisis point where, if they weren't taking anti-depressants, they'd probably jump off a bridge. So yes, I think in terms of crisis points, therapy is very necessary, and medication is probably a really good idea. To consistently maintain it after the space of maximum...about two years, I think is very dangerous. 'Cos it builds a dependency, whether it's chemical or...emotional. Whether that's as a result of either pharmacology, or going to have therapy. I don't believe in long-term therapy.

However, he expressed disapproval of the way in which people come to depend upon therapy long-term; he also described depression as a 'way of being' and did not agree that it should be considered to be a 'disease' that must be cured. Again then, his account also echoes the naturalness discourse; depression, for Chris, should constitute a *natural* part of an individual's self or character rather than something that needs to be 'artificially' corrected by an external source.

Beth – earlier in her interview – said that she did not 'believe in depression' before explaining further:

Beth (23, female): I've never needed to take [anti-depressants]. If it's to do with sorting out this chemical imbalance...as a short-term thing, maybe, but then if it doesn't get fixed then they're just continually taking the pills and obviously it's not...doing the job. I think you've just got to force yourself to...to get out there really, no matter how unhappy you are. You've just to force yourself to do it.

LH: *You said you don't believe in depression...*

Beth (23, female): Well I think there are like extreme cases where people do have a problem, but I think that like, as a nation, a lot of people say they're depressed, but they're only as depressed as I've ever felt, but I'd never call myself depressed, even if I felt depressed. Yeah, I think there's extremes, there will be a few people, but I think some people just jump into it, and...they will say it. I think it's a worrying thing...like, in other cultures, they might be a bit happier because they've got a simple life, and I don't think they have depressed people in those societies.

It's like we've invented the term. I mean, there will be extremes where people do have problems, but there are people in between. Like, I could go to the doctor and say I was depressed, and he might give me a pill, but I don't think I need one. Do you know what I mean? So there may be people on the borderline, where there may be a different way of looking at it. Because I think we all feel sad sometimes.

Beth described the growing incidence of depression as 'a worrying thing', but also emphasised that a small number of people are 'extreme cases' who have a real 'problem'. Rather than seeking assistance from therapy or medication, she felt that most unhappy people should 'force' themselves to 'get out there'; again, this suggests that 'natural' means of regaining happiness are preferable here.

Tom, Chris and Beth in all of these three accounts – as well as many other respondents – are also positioning themselves in the *biological* discourse, where they recognise that whilst for most people, therapy and medication are not necessary during unhappy times in life (as they are 'unnatural' means of recovery), there are nevertheless a small number of cases that are characterised by genuine 'illness' which is biological or physiological in nature and therefore therapeutic or pharmacological intervention is acceptable.

Although these accounts illustrate a general scepticism towards the therapy industry (and these are also representative of the attitudes of many of my other respondents), the majority of people nevertheless situated themselves within therapeutic discourse; that is, experience of happiness was, for them, a specifically *individual* experience, closely related to therapeutic precepts of self-care and self-knowledge, which are both qualities or values that are strongly advocated by the therapy industry and self-help literature. It is this to which the chapter will now turn.

Therapeutic happiness

An individual experience

Many of the people I interviewed considered happiness to be something that is to be sought and experienced by the individual, and thus as a very personal, subjective experience, as opposed to anything social or communal. Beth commented, for example, that 'you've got to find it yourself' and that 'it's about you':

> LH: *What do you think happiness actually is?*
>
> Beth (23, female): Well it's something... I think you've got to find it yourself, haven't you... it's about you. And it's about accepting your situation, and making the best of whatever it is. I think if you're continually striving and you don't accept where you are, you could be really miserable. So I think it's just kind of accepting... where you are, and just appreciating all the things that you do have. Instead of worrying about what you don't have.

Her account suggests that to be happy, an individual must *evaluate* their personal circumstances, reflect upon all of the different aspects of their life, but also accept what they have. It is only when the individual has done so that they can appreciate themselves and what they have, and to therefore be happy.

Denise also described happiness as something subjective and unique, by talking about the way in which each individual is likely to have their own 'version' of it (and thus also positioned herself within the uniqueness discourse discussed in the preceding chapter):

> Denise (46, female): I think different people like different things, you know, there are those of us who would – if money were no object – choose to holiday in a hot place, those of us who would choose to go trekking round cities, those who want to be with people, those who don't... I think there must be almost as many variations on happiness as there are people.

This comment points to the perceived importance of personal *choice* in contemporary neoliberal societies; that is to say that how one goes about achieving happiness is considered to be their individual preference, and unconstrained by any other sources outside the self, despite the fact that the accounts of happiness that respondents gave me shared many similarities.

Similarly, Lizzie talked about her experience of happiness in relation to the individual autonomy and choice that she has over it:

LH: Would you say that happiness is a short-term feeling, or more of a longer-lasting state?

Lizzie (25, female): For me, probably a longer-lasting state. I can't say that everything's going right all of the time, but as long as most things are going well for me, that would generally make me a happy person. I think I've got a lot of choice in that as well. And you know, say I'm not happy because I...I don't know, I'm hungover or something [laughs], obviously that's going to be part of it as well, but you know, that was a sacrifice I made the night before! You know, if I decide I want to talk to my sister on the phone more often, I think that's a choice I can actually make, and I should be able to change it. I mean, not everything's going to be perfect, like I can't easily go to New Zealand or go to see my mum in South Africa, but I can try and make the most of the things that I've got now...obviously with the income that I have as well, to change the way I'm feeling. You know, if I don't feel as though I've got out enough to do enough exercise or something, I can wake up tomorrow morning and decide that I'm going to do this, or do that. So I think it's got a huge amount to do with choice.

Her account initially suggests that her happiness is rarely influenced or affected by external or social factors. It could be argued that she positions herself as 'reflexive' here (Beck, 1992, Giddens, 1991), with the capacity to exercise choice over how she lives her life. However, she also acknowledges that there may be some barriers to this reflexivity, such as difficulties in being able to visit her family abroad regularly.

Chloe, when discussing her experience of happiness in relation to being in love, talked about the way in which a loving relationship in the past had provided her with happiness in the form of self-confidence. She also stressed, echoing advice that is given in self-help literature, the importance of having happiness 'within yourself'. Not only does this resonate with the idea that the body or self is a container for emotions (Lupton, 1998), but her account had similarities with advice given by Robert Holden in *Happiness Now! Timeless Wisdom for Feeling Good Fast* (2007:67): 'unless you're happy with yourself, you will not be happy'. She felt that it is imperative that one should always be happy with oneself rather than relying on a partner or lover for happiness, as this provides a safeguard against intensified misery in the potentiality that a relationship should end. Again, this resonates with Holden's advice: 'The world does not have your happiness; you have your happiness. [...] happiness is not outside you' (2007:45).

> Chloe (26, female): I had a three-year relationship with someone who I loved and loved me back, and it was lovely, and it was the constant of that security of just having... and I know that during that time I had a lot of confidence because I just had him there, and I knew he thought I was the bee's knees. And when I came out of it, I was of course like, 'yeah, I'm single!', but I was also... there was a few years where I didn't find that again, and I was like 'urgh', and what I learnt was, you have to find that [happiness] within yourself. So... I think it can be short-term [gasps], lust and fun, and it can have a long-time security, but I think you should always, always, always have it within yourself. And I think people who rely on that definitely don't have it, because nowadays, relationships end. You know, they might go on for forty years, but they ultimately do end, so I think if you have it in yourself... you can bring so much to the other person.

This account has similarities with Hazleden's (2003) observation that in order to be fulfilled and happy, many Westerners believe that one must learn to 'love' their self. This should take priority over seeking love from others, and is a key aspect of therapeutic discourse. The discourse also suggests that happiness is something whose source is *internal*, that is, bodily in some way, or experienced at the level of consciousness, thus again, rendering the experience of happiness very personal and unique. It is in this way, then, that the therapeutic or individualisation discourse intersects with those of naturalness and uniqueness.

Whilst these four accounts all tell different stories, one thing that they all have in common is that they all assume that it is the level of the individual – rather than the group, or society, for instance – at which happiness is always experienced. This individualistic view of happiness was also evident when I was asked by two respondents subsequent to their interviews – and independently of one another – how I hoped to make sense of the interview data, as they felt that what they had just told me in relation to their conceptions and experiences of happiness was extremely subjective and personal. This way of describing happiness is not distinctly 'therapeutic' per se; however, such a discourse of individualisation is intimately linked with the therapeutic narrative, inasmuch as the latter is characterised by a way of looking at the world in which the individual, the self and self-sufficiency take precedence over communitarian values, and it is the self which takes centre stage in the therapeutic enterprise and in advice literature. Indeed, as discussed in Chapter 2, therapeutic discourse has also been shown to obscure the social dimension of the human self, and it is an individual, and perhaps psychological conception of the self, like that adopted by self-help literature (Rimke, 2000) that takes precedence in people's accounts of happiness here, over and above ideas around human interdependence.

Related to the idea that happiness is experienced at the level of the individual is that where it is understood as something that is internally experienced, at the level of consciousness. Chloe, for example, described happiness as 'an internal steadiness' and a 'voice inside you':

> Chloe (26, female): I don't think your happiness should come from external...motivations, or material goods, or people...I think they can, and you'll probably get happy for a bit, but if you rely on that, you can always come back down again. I think it should always be an internal sort of...steadiness, and motivation, because that will never go, that voice inside you will never go...whereas Manolo Blahniks will go out of season [laughs]. I mean, I'm saying this but if I go out tomorrow and buy a really cute All Saints jacket, I'd be really pleased. But I try and personally concentrate myself on having an inner happiness where the outside events are good and bad, because I know that's the thing that will always be there.

She identified benefits of making sense of happiness in this way; having an 'inner happiness' is something that an individual can always have, which may not be the case with happiness that is gained from the 'outside' world (for example, from shopping and consumption). It is such self-sufficiency (which is also advocated by the self-help literature) that is likely to enable the individual to maximise his or her happiness; indeed, for Hazleden (2003), self-sufficiency is understood as paramount to 'forming a healthy relationship with the self' (2003:421). Rather than channel one's energies into caring for others, therapeutic or 'psy' discourses encourage investment in the care for one's self; it is this that allows for the cultivation of a positive relationship with the self, which is in turn most conducive to happiness. Chloe's account also implies that happiness is something 'real' or tangible that exists as a part of one's body that can then be deployed by the individual whenever necessary (which would indeed not be feasible in the case of happiness from external sources). This resonates with the discourse of elusiveness explored in the previous chapter, where those situating themselves within this consider happiness to be a part of the self, yet seemingly elusive due to its embodied and often unconscious nature.

Sophie also talked about the experience of *un*happiness in relation to psychological or internal ideas such as paranoia and one's inner thoughts:

> Sophie (22, female): I feel as though I could never be completely happy in life, because you always want what you can't have. Whether you've got what you wanted in the first place, you'll want more than that. So you're never going to be satisfied. And I know that even if the thing that comes along that makes you happy, even when you get what you thought was going to make you happy, it will make you happy for a very short time, but you'll still go back to being low again ... you know, you might get the relationship you want but then you might be paranoid that it's not going to work out. And a lot of people, they ... make it reality. Like, you might say to yourself in your head ... you're thinking, getting a bit paranoid, that you're not happy with your life, everyone else has a boyfriend, their lives are great, mine's not. But they're not, other people are probably thinking the same thing! But as soon as you start saying that you start to make it seem like reality. It might not become a reality but you're making it out to be something it's not. It's like, if you're in a room and you're not talking to anyone, you might think 'no-one's talking to me' ... well of course they won't talk to you if you don't talk to them! You're making it a reality.

Echoing Chloe's suggestion that happiness is an internal 'voice', Sophie made sense of feelings of *un*happiness through the idea of an internal 'conversation' that one might have with oneself, in which one would evaluate the extent to which they are happy. She also highlighted the idea that one's internal thoughts can become 'reality' and that living one's life in a reality constituted of such thoughts could give rise to further unhappiness. Her account therefore suggests that a major source of the experience and the modification of one's state of happiness is cerebral, emerging from an internal dialogue. Not only does this converge with the discourse of elusiveness in the same way as that of Chloe above, but it is also a direct illustration of the way in which Sophie (and indeed, Chloe) has situated herself in therapeutic discourse; 'talking' with oneself about how one should make sense of particular aspects of one's life is a form of self-care that is strongly advocated by the therapeutic enterprise and self-help literature (Hazleden, 2003, Rimke, 2000).

'Working' on the self

In keeping with the therapeutic ideal of the paramount importance of the self, many of the accounts that my interviewees gave suggested that 'working' on oneself, or self-care, is necessary for the achievement or the experience of happiness. In other words, they talked about the way in which one ought to take *control* over their lives and their inner thoughts, strive to achieve personal 'goals' and be proactive about making changes to any aspects of their life that they feel is a source of misery, or that is not giving them happiness.

Thus, Denise reflected upon her positive experience of having counselling, and attributed this to the fact that she was 'doing something proactive about things':

> LH: *Some people take anti-depressants or see therapists or counsellors in order to make themselves happier these days – what do you think of this?*
>
> Denise (46, female): As somebody who takes anti-depressants and who has seen a counsellor in the past year...for me, the gobby mare that I am, it's good to talk, it's good to feel that I'm doing something proactive about things. I don't think talking therapies...cognitive behaviour therapy...medication, or whatever, in themselves, make you happy. They're not happy pills per se.

> But I think they can help... a combination of all those things can
> help you get to a place where you can start to move forward. But
> I don't think it's the pills or the therapy itself that in a vacuum
> would make you happy. But I would say it's a good thing.
> *LH: Do you feel that they helped you?*
> Denise (46, female): Yes, they've definitely helped me... again,
> I don't think it was the pills, I don't think it was the ther-
> apy... but for me, it was all of those things, and helping me to
> change how I felt about myself and.. give me an opportunity to
> see what I could do differently. And some bits I can, some bits
> I can't.

She talked about the way in which this experience made her feel happier; this was not due to the therapy that she had received or the
tablets that she had taken in and of themselves, but rather the way in
which drawing on these enabled her to change and improve her *self-
perception* after having experienced a range of problems, thus deeming
this process a form of 'work' on the self. Denise also equated feeling happy with 'moving forward', which implies that she subscribes
to this discourse that views life as a 'project' or 'journey' during
which happiness can be sought and which needs to be persistently
monitored. This is a way of thinking that is strongly advocated by
the therapy industry and which forms part of therapeutic discourse
(see Hazleden, 2003:421). For example, psychologist Tom G. Stevens
advises, in *You Can Choose To Be Happy: 'Rise Above' Anxiety, Anger and
Depression* (2010), that

> life is a journey through time and space. In this journey, we are
> explorers, and each of us finds our own unique path. In our own
> private journeys we will visit many places – some happy and some
> not. Our goal is to learn, create and be as happy as possible.
>
> (Stevens, 2010:45)

This is also a technique that people engage in which Rimke (2000)
suggests is central to the political programmes of neoliberal societies, in allowing people to be 'effective' citizens who are able to
take responsibility for themselves. Thus, her account suggests that
to be happy requires a degree of 'work' or self-care (again, a fundamental precept of the self-help industry); that is, proactiveness about

changing an unfavourable situation, which would in turn alter one's personal outlook and level of self-esteem.

Nick also used the idea of 'moving forward' with regard to his happiness, particularly in relation to his work as an actor and television writer:

> LH: *Could you tell me a bit more about the way in which you get happiness from your work? What is it about being challenged that makes you feel good?*
>
> Nick (25, male): Well... sense of achievement, so when someone says 'well done, you're good at something', that makes me feel happy. But it's also... Using my emotions, I'm quite an emotional person, that makes me happy. Because it means that I'm getting them out, and dealing with stuff. Anything that makes me feel like I'm improving, moving forward, rather than just sitting still, makes me happy. But, like, different areas of my work make me happy in different ways... [...] With acting you have to audition and there are lots of different... variants as to if you get the part. Like, they might want someone taller, fatter, anything, whereas with writing, you kind of make a product and then you give the product out, and it's coming from your voice. So it's like when you're telling part of your own story, when you feel like you're being authentic... if that makes sense? If you're being authentic to yourself... you're kind of... being true to yourself. You know, that you know you're not compromising yourself. The times when I felt most unhappy are the times when I felt like I was compromising myself.

He, like Denise, also suggested that being proactive (or 'dealing with stuff') by using his emotions is important for being happy, and that it is important to progress – or 'work' – rather than to 'sit still'. He also talked about the happiness that he has gained from writing, where he felt that he was given the opportunity to be 'authentic' or 'true' to himself. This suggests that he has probably taken time in the past to reflect on the nature of his 'self' in order that he is able to recognise authenticity when it is experienced; this could be considered to be another form of self-care or 'work', in that it would enable him to get to 'know' himself and would not require him to behave in a way that may be discordant with his own character. Talking about his self in this way (that is, the idea of being 'true' to oneself, or 'compromising' oneself) also resonates with the constitution of the self adopted in self-help literature, whereby one sets up a *relation* to their self that is ontologically separate (Hazleden, 2003; see Chapter 2 for general discussion on this). That is, Nick described being at his happiest when he is being 'true' to himself, and thus, when his relationship with his self was at its most positive.

Chloe specifically acknowledged that one ought to 'work at' their happiness. Reiterating that discussed in the previous section of happiness being internal, she identified the benefits of this, particularly with regard to the fact that she is single and often spends time alone. For her, 'working' at her happiness allows her to enjoy this time:

> Chloe (26, female): I just really believe that [happiness] is something that comes within yourself, and you should work at it just as much as you work at everything else ... just as much as you work at ... I don't know, your abs, or something like that! Or your job, or your relationship with your mum and dad ... I think it's something inside you that you should work at. And I think that's a big thing about being single as well ... I think time alone is so important, and the thing I'm most grateful for is the fact that ... I'm happy to hang out with myself, like the fact that I get on with myself.

What is interesting about each of the above three accounts (and indeed, many of the others that concern 'work' on the self) is that the respondents talk about their 'selves' as though they are *separate* entities to themselves as individuals. That is, they set up a relation that they have with their selves, so that they as individuals are able to reflect on their selves as though they are another person. This again, is one way in which self-help manuals commonly characterise the self. Indeed, these accounts resonate with the model of selfhood that Rebecca Hazleden (2003) found to be used in a range of relationship manuals (see Chapter 3 for discussion of this); the self is constituted as being '*ontologically separate* from itself' (Hazleden, 2003:416), in order that it can be 'worked' on. Thus essentially, by situating themselves within therapeutic discourse, these individuals appear to gain happiness by cultivating *relationships* with their selves that they are then able to work on, bring 'forward' and ultimately feel happy with. As Hazleden points out, having a high regard for one's self in this way, and 'getting on with oneself', as Chloe says is key to personal fulfilment and happiness.

Taking control of one's life is another way in which the self can be 'worked' on (Hazleden, 2003). Chloe, talked about the way in which she takes control of her happiness, and that she feels that this is an aspect of her personality:

> LH: *Do you feel happy at the moment?*
>
> Chloe (26, female): Erm...yes, I do. But...that's probably hugely to do with the personality that I think I have, which is that I take control of my own happiness...like, it's very rare that I would let myself get...that down. I mean...like, I broke up with my year-long boyfriend about a month ago, and my girl friends were like 'oh my god, we'll come round with ice cream and vodka!', and I got a bit, like, teary that day, I walked away from his house and I was like [makes sad face], and I rang my mum and I was a bit teary on the phone, and my mum said something which is like the way she's brought me up, which is probably what's in me, and she said 'you know, in a month, you'll be over this, so why don't you just be over it now?'...and I literally haven't been upset since. [...] I was like, actually I am going to be fine with this. And I'm gonna be more fine if I think myself there.

Whilst this also resonates with the positive thinking discourse discussed in Chapter 3, Chloe highlighted the way in which taking control in this way ensures that she feels a minimal amount of unhappiness. She therefore 'works' on herself, in monitoring her happiness levels. The 'thinking' herself to happiness that she talked about, then, could be considered a technology of the self (Foucault, 1988); it is a technique that she utilises in order to regulate her happiness. However, whilst she suggests that happiness is something that one can easily control, she also attributes this to her personality and her upbringing (by describing her mother's similar outlook), thus implying that this is something relatively fixed and innate. Furthermore, suggesting that her attitude towards happiness is also inherited from her parents demonstrates that she also makes sense of this through a more biological framework.

Similarly, Martin described the way in which a *loss* of control – due to a recent car accident, burglary and change in employment that he had experienced – led to a feeling of immense *un*happiness, loss of confidence and anxiety. Although the quote below is about confidence – an aspect of self-knowledge, which will be explored in the next section – what Martin says about losing control relates to a lack of ability to 'work' on oneself:

> Martin (32, male): I've found myself in the last year being tremendously anxious. [...] I guess you could say that my confidence has obviously taken a blow, because...I lost control of the car...lost control at some point of my career, I thought...lost control of my house, because people came in and took my stuff when I was in bed...so yeah, a lot of feelings of loss of control. The thing with the Japanese company where I worked, which didn't work out – I was forced to find another job but it was a scary time, it was a form of loss of control. 'Cos I used to be tremendously confident in my jobs and in myself, probably too much, I was probably too aggressive, saying things that were too arrogant...So yeah, a number of events which could all be put on the same denominator, the loss of control, whether it's over your steering wheel, over your job, over your house. And yeah, I guess that sort of erodes...not your confidence as a man maybe, but your sense of being in control of life. It makes the world seem like a much more scary place. I think it's just something you have to work through, you know.

He equated the loss of control with a loss of confidence in himself; his account suggests that to be in control of life is a normal and desirable quality and suggested that in order to regain this quality, he would need to 'work through' these negative emotions, thus directly suggesting that some kind of inner reflection and 'work' on himself would be required.

Thus it can be seen that the idea that happiness can be gained via 'work' on oneself is widely held, and forms a fundamental part of therapeutic discourse. Individuals who do so seek to examine their selves and attempt to cultivate a relationship with their self that they set up as being ontologically separate, as is often done in self-help literature (see Hazleden, 2003); if one does this successfully, this may be manifested in a feeling of possession of a greater degree of control over their life. Individuals who feel that they lack control, such as Martin, may therefore be considered to have a weaker, or less 'healthy' relationship with their self (2003:421). That is to say, a loss of control and the occurrence of unpredictable or unplanned events may result in an individual feeling less able to have a high level of regard for themselves.

'Knowing' oneself

Closely related to the idea that one ought to 'work' on or 'care' for their self in order to be happy is that of the way in which one should 'know' oneself; these are two of the most fundamental and central self-oriented precepts of therapeutic culture and discourse, and is another central dimension of self-help texts. As Hazleden says, 'the ethical *telos* of the books is therefore that of an individual who is self-regarding, and who has mastered the arts of self-knowledge and emotional self-discipline' (2003:424). It could also be argued that the seeking of self-knowledge is inextricably bound up with self-regulation and the governing of the self, in order that people are able to be 'effective' citizens (Foucault, 1988, Rimke, 2000).

This idea was expressed by some interviewees, who highlighted the way in which self-confidence or self-awareness is important for being happy, such as Danielle and Lizzie:

LH: Do you think we need to feel confident in order to feel happy?
Danielle (26, female): Er, well confident in who you are, not necessarily extrovert or outwardly... confident. I think you can be shy with new people in social circumstances, or at work, but still be a happy person. [...] ... yeah, just being confident in who you are and that you've got friends who you like and who appreciate you the way you are. I think that makes you happy.

LH: What do you think happiness actually is?
Lizzie (25, female): Erm... I think it's feeling... maybe confident... with yourself and your surroundings. [...]
LH: Do you think confidence and happiness are linked?
Lizzie (25, female): I think to a certain extent, yes. I think if you're happy in yourself, that that naturally comes out through the person that you are. As well, I think that you do have a lot more confidence too... because you're content with yourself. Well, not content with yourself, but maybe you're... over-content, because that's just being happy with yourself. And I think that naturally comes through. And the way that you talk, the way that you

act, the way that you speak … so yeah, I'd say definitely, that can come through.

Self-confidence, another prominent aspect of therapeutic culture, is, according to self-help writer Napoleon Hill (2002), an outcome of self-knowledge: 'Self-confidence is the product of knowledge. Know yourself, know how much you know (and how little), why you know it, and how you are going to use it' (2002:225). In both of the above accounts, a happy person is understood as someone who is confident with *who they are*; that is to say, someone who possesses some kind of knowledge of their identity and character, and for whom positive evaluations from others would be likely to reinforce this knowledge. Lizzie also described the way in which one's confidence can be displayed in their behaviour, thus constituting a major element of their personality, which she also described as natural. Therefore, whilst Lizzie feels that confidence – and heightened self-knowledge – is integral to happiness, she also views this as something *natural*, and thus produced internally for the individual to experience.

Denise also highlighted the importance of being comfortable with oneself to be happy and suggested that this is a more important factor than one's outward, physical appearance:

LH: *Do you think beauty and appearance can be linked to happiness?*
Denise (46, female): [pause] Probably, yes. I mean, I think most of us at some point focus on some aspect of our physical appearance, whether it's 'I could do with losing a few pounds', or 'I need to get my nails done', or whatever. You know, something relatively small. Or other things more major, a little bit of surgery or whatever. I think it's of concern and it affects the happiness of that person, but I don't think most other people look at someone and think 'oh, she'd be so much prettier if she was blonde', or 'she'd be so much prettier if she was a 38 double-J instead of being blatantly a 34B, how dare she leave the house like that!' [laughs]. But I think it's about how you feel, rather than how the world sees you. There are certain images, especially in this country and the Western world … But I think people, when they're looking at somebody else, what they find attractive or whatever is people who are comfortable with themselves. But I think we … we forget that and we think 'oh, she can do that, because

whatever', but it's about being happy with yourself, 'I'm happy with myself, I don't have to lose that extra couple of pounds'.

She talks about the way in which physical appearance is considered by some to be important on a social level, but then goes on to emphasise that for most people, confidence on a deeper, more internal level is more important, and that 'it's about being happy with yourself'. Thus, despite a preoccupation in the media with appearance, what is actually important is the possession of a certain level of self-knowledge in order that one can appreciate oneself. Like with the idea of 'working' on oneself then, to 'know' oneself requires that the individual 'loves' him or herself, and successfully cultivates a *positive* relationship with their 'ontologically separate' self (see Hazleden, 2003). It is only when such a positive relationship has been established and can be subsequently maintained that a sense of both self-confidence and happiness can be achieved.

Denise's account also illustrates the importance for happiness of the symbolic interactionist constitution of the self. Her statement that 'it's about how you feel, rather than how the world sees you. I think people, when they're looking at somebody else, what they find attractive or whatever is people who are comfortable with themselves', may initially suggest that the source of happiness is the 'I', rather than the 'me' (Mead, 1934). Happiness is brought about by oneself, and how 'comfortable' they are about themselves, rather than by others. However, a happy 'me' may be achieved by displaying to others that one is comfortable with oneself, and that they possess a degree of self-knowledge.

The idea of *understanding oneself* also arose in a number of interviews. Chris talked about the way in which moving to the United Kingdom from Canada several months previously had provided him with a better understanding of himself and had allowed him to 'define' who he is, and this for him was a source of happiness:

> Chris (46, male): What's really interesting, and what makes me happy, is that when you're outside of your culture, you learn what it is to be of your own culture, because you can see it by difference. So it actually defines you. And Canadians are consistently looking for definition, because they sit in this limbo ... there's a cultural and national obsession about what it is

to be Canadian. [...] the thing is, that when you leave...all that you're familiar with, you're forced to like, finally define who you are. And so that actually makes me happy, bizarre as that may seem.

Lizzie also felt that the increased self-understanding that she had gained from her relationship with her sister since she moved to the United Kingdom from New Zealand was a source of happiness:

> LH: *Would you say that it's important to have good relationships with family and friends in order to be happy?*
>
> Lizzie (25, female): Yeah I think so, I think that's probably the thing that would make you most happy...I think I'm a lot happier with the way I am around my sister, especially since I moved over here, we've got a much better relationship than we ever did back in New Zealand. Spending more time with her over here and understanding who she is as a person, even though I didn't have to, but she's blood...I feel a lot happier in myself, because I understand who I am more, and who my sister is more. And because we've only got each other as well, over here...well, we've got aunties and uncles and things like that, but we've almost recovered ourselves over here...and we've got a much better relationship. I'm starting understand her as a person, that's taken a bit of time and effort actually, because I do see that we're very different in the way that we are, our lives are almost completely different. So I think something like that can make you happier.

Thus, Chris and Lizzie both gained happiness from an increased self-understanding that they had obtained after moving to the United Kingdom from abroad. Although Chris expressed that gaining happiness in this way was 'bizarre' and perhaps unusual, it could indeed be said that – in the same way as the others who position themselves in this discourse – it is the increased self-knowledge, the ability to hold himself in higher regard, and therefore the cultivation of a positive relationship with his self (Hazleden, 2003) that has instilled this feeling. In other words he – as well as others who have expressed this – has gained a feeling of happiness from knowing or defining who he is. For Lizzie, such a reflexive relationship is also present. By understanding her sister's identity, she has also learnt about her own, thus enhancing her self-knowledge.

Martin, on the other hand, talked about the way in which he has experienced *un*happiness because of a 'struggle' or inability to 'find' himself and be confident:

> Martin (32, male): I think my current relationship has triggered a bunch of emotions which I'm not familiar with, which I'm scared of in some ways. Yeah, my life has definitely changed a lot in the last... and that's fine, I just wish it wouldn't make it so difficult, because I feel like I've struggled more nowadays than I used to...
>
> *LH: Struggle with these emotions, or with life generally?*
>
> Martin (32, male): Struggle in terms of... finding yourself, maybe being happy, being confident, thinking more... yeah. Nowadays I just feel stressed out all the time, I didn't used to have that. I ask myself why, where does it come from, where's the problem, why can't I just go back to... you know. It doesn't necessarily mean I want to live the life I had two years ago, although it certainly was simpler [laughs], and only involved going out and earning money, getting drunk, having fun. So yeah, everything's become much more of a question.

He introspectively described the way in which his relationship with his girlfriend over the past year – which had also led to a change in lifestyle for him – had led to an experience of unfamiliar emotions, which he saw to be a cause of great fear. Thus, by setting up a relation of his self to itself, as is frequently done in self-help literature and which is also a major aspect of therapeutic, or 'psy' discourse (Hazleden, 2003), he described this inability to find himself – or his 'loss' of self, which had led to a feeling of anxiety. He sought to deal with this by asking himself questions, and engaging in internal dialogue; he sought to 'work' on himself in order to identify the cause of the problem. Happiness for Martin could therefore only be regained if he were able to obtain more self-knowledge, and if he was therefore able improve his relationship with his self, and have higher regard for it. Martin, then, in drawing on major aspects of self-help culture in giving his account of unhappiness (that is, conceiving of his self as something separate that he then felt able to turn back on and 'work' on through internal dialogue, and expressing a wish for greater self-knowledge) also situated himself within therapeutic discourse.

Lizzie talked about the way in which her work was a source of happiness for her, particularly in relation to the fact that she now knows what she would like to do with her life in terms of a career:

> Lizzie (25, female): I think [my career] is going really well for me at the moment. About six months ago I was in a secretarial role for the Director of Communications at [government department] and when he got promoted, I had the opportunity to move, to get rid of the secretarial role, and start at the bottom of press and marketing which is an area that I really want to get into. So I'm kind of in the process at the moment of...even though I get called a press and marketing officer, I'm almost a little bit below that role, but I'm being trained up by people that I really respect a lot, and have good relationships with all my colleagues...they're kind of training me up at the moment and they're really helping me and mentoring me and kind of showing me the ropes for the things that I need to do to be able to get up to the next level in my career. So even though I'm not quite there yet, I'm at a stage of my life where I finally know what I want to do...for the moment, and I'm achieving it at the moment.

It is clear from Lizzie's account that she had previously engaged in much personal reflection on what she would like to do with her life, and that having arrived at a decision about this – and therefore furthering her self-knowledge – has led to a feeling of happiness. This furthering of her self-knowledge is something that strengthens one's relationship with their self, and gives rise to being happy.

Similarly, Martin also felt that to be happy requires knowledge that one's life is going 'in the right direction':

> Martin (32, male): ...nowadays most of my happiness comes from being with somebody that I love, or really like, who I feel loved by, and understood by, and you get a sense that you're realising your potential I suppose. That your life is heading in the right direction...

Again, by expressing that happiness is 'realising your potential', Martin's account suggests he had undertaken some reflection that allowed him to understand what his potential was. Thus, like for Lizzie, Martin gained happiness from an increased self-knowledge in which an understanding of what he wanted from life was paramount. Thinking about life in terms of 'direction' also relates to the therapeutic ideal that life is a 'project' or a 'journey' in which one is able to 'work' on themselves in order to maximise their happiness (Rose, 1996). Therefore individuals who situate themselves in therapeutic discourse appear to engage in this kind of reflection throughout their lives to ensure that they remain personally fulfilled; this reflection is also a form of 'work' on the self that enables the individual to take *control* over their life and self, to gain self-knowledge and to ultimately achieve happiness.

Therefore when situating oneself in therapeutic discourse, knowing oneself is another fundamental way in which happiness can be achieved and maximised. Being confident and comfortable with oneself is considered necessary, as well as the possession of a sense of personal identity and self; that is, a 'healthy', positive relationship with oneself (Hazleden, 2003) is imperative. Lacking this relationship, and an absence of self-knowledge, may bring about a feeling of anxiety and one may therefore feel inclined to 'work' on oneself, or engage in internal dialogue with oneself (or draw on another technology of the self (see Foucault, 1988)) in an attempt to regain this and find happiness.

Unhappiness, introspection and everyday life events

Some interviewees positioned themselves in therapeutic discourse by describing unhappy, but often mundane, everyday experiences, using introspective and psychological language, thus transforming them – as discussed at the start of the chapter – into emotion-laden events. This is another aspect of neoliberal, therapeutic culture that Rose (1996) and Furedi (2004) identify (for further discussion of this, see section entitled 'Self, identity and personhood' in Chapter 2).

Gillian talked in a very general and hypothetical – but nevertheless introspective – way about how she would deal with feelings of depression if they ever arose, though this was not in relation to any particular experience per se. She stressed that she would not take medication, but that she would want to experience the depression (or indeed, 'turmoil', as she described it):

> Gillian (45, female): I personally, if I was going through a depressed stage and the doctor said 'here are some anti-depressants', I don't think I'd take them, I think I'd be strong enough to get through it. And I think I'd probably want to cry my eyes out, I'd want to get it out of my system. Want to go through the turmoil, knowing that I was gonna come out the other side, do you know what I mean?

The idea that she should want to 'come out the other side' suggests that, for Gillian, life is again considered a kind of 'journey' on which a period of depression might feature, thus resonating with therapeutic discourse. Recovery from such a period would then be made sense of as a later point on that journey, a point at which one would have removed the depression from their 'system'. Depression therefore, is seen as not only something real and tangible, but also corporeal, and experienced as a bodily process in the same way as happiness may be construed. The idea that the body is a *container* for the emotions is used here (Lupton, 1998); depression is something that needs to be removed from this container, or from one's 'system'.

Mark also described his actual experience of depression and anti-depressant use introspectively, using words like 'anxious' and considering himself to be in a 'dip'; that is, words which were previously confined to the realm of psychotherapy and psychology (or the 'psy sciences') (Furedi, 2004). He felt reluctant to start taking medication for his depression again, due to the feelings of anxiety and misery that they had caused him previously and, instead, hoped that a man with whom he had had recent correspondence via an online dating website and whom he was due to meet face-to-face would distract him from his depression:

> Mark (41, male): I actually cancelled a doctor's appointment this afternoon because of wanting to go on anti-depressants, and then I decided against it. I'm prone to depression anyway, and again, that's to do with chemical imbalances I think. […] I spent years on anti-depressants. And I … I'm being truthful here, anti-depressants gave me a bit of an edge that made me feel anxious.

[...] I need to get out of the dip that I'm in at the moment, and...fingers crossed, Paul [man from the Internet] will be a way to do that. I'm not suggesting that Paul will be the fix, but he'll be a distraction to get me out of the dip that I was in, whether it comes to anything or not. So I decided against going to the doctor to get prescribed anti-depressants because they make me feel anxious and miserable.

He attributed his depression to 'chemical imbalances' which again suggests that for him, as with Gillian, depression is something biological and physiological. That is, both he and Gillian situate themselves within a biological discourse of unhappiness. Whilst people describe depression using introspective and 'emotional' language, situating oneself in therapeutic discourse also gives rise to the idea that depression, like happiness when considered in relation to the 'naturalness' discourse, is considered to be biological, produced and experienced within the body. Furthermore, this discourse of unhappiness promotes the idea that the bodily experience of depression may be understood to 'contaminate' one's happiness in some way (by perhaps limiting the production of serotonin) and thus causing a feeling of misery.

Other respondents used such introspective and emotional language in describing everyday – and sometimes mundane – experiences. Martin, for example, talked about difficult times that he had experienced in his previous job, and the words 'traumatising', 'messed me up' and 'suffer' featured in his account of this:

Martin (32, male): I signed on with a Japanese company, first as a contractor, but within three weeks they made me permanent, but in the end that totally didn't work out, so that was a very bad experience. It was quite traumatising as well, because I'd never had such conflict at work...Japanese companies are very different, you have to be in at nine o'clock. If you get in at one past nine a few times, they'll know and they'll send you a written letter saying you could be subjected to disciplinary...very, very tough. And yeah, I think that kind of messed me up as well, because it made me very fearful of people I work with, because they might be nice to you, but – at least at that place where I worked – but then they sort of...completely did a U-turn. For a long time it made me really suffer…so then I moved to [current workplace], which I guess was a really good thing…

Alex, too, talked about having to move away from his home town at the age of 16, and having to start attending a new college in an unfamiliar place; he described the 'panic attacks' that he experienced at this time:

> Alex (25, male): I really didn't cope [with moving away] very well. I think I have a tendency to bottle things up. So yeah…first of all I just got really, really angry inside, but I didn't really express it much. Yeah, I really didn't cope with that, I just got really really angry, and frustrated. Actually it caused…in the end, I started having panic attacks…I think it was because of this, whatever it was, boiling up inside me, and I wasn't expressing it.

In both cases, the events described – experiencing conflict in the workplace and relocating to a new area – are not unusual experiences in the contemporary West; nevertheless, both Martin and Alex described their experiences as 'traumatising' and anger-inducing. That is, they both described their experiences using 'psy' vocabulary (Furedi, 2004). For Martin, his unhappiness was something psychological with which he 'suffered'; Alex talked about the way in which he needed to 'cope' with it, but found this difficult, to the point of experiencing panic attacks, a medical or psychological term used increasingly in Western culture to describe a highly intense period of fear and anxiety (NHS Choices, 2013). Like with that of Mark and Gillian, the language that Alex uses in his account suggests that he situates himself within a biological discourse as well as that of the therapeutic; here, anxiety or unhappiness is reified as something *real* and *tangible* that can be 'bottled up' within oneself. Alex, too, then, draws upon the idea of the body being a container for the emotions (Lupton, 1998), in which they can be 'controlled' in this way. He also utilised a fluidity metaphor (Lupton, 1998) in talking about the way in which his feeling of anger, which was located internally, 'boiled up' as it grew in intensity.

Martin also talked about the experience of a panic attack – albeit a hypothetical one – in another account, with regard to how he would feel about potentially becoming a father:

LH: *Do you think that marriage and having children is something you could look to as a potentially happy time?*

Martin (32, male): Yeah, I think so. I think you enter a different dimension, you have this nice cosy feeling of having a family, yeah it would be nice. But scary as well, like, last summer I thought that my girlfriend might be pregnant [...] but it didn't happen. Probably a good thing. But the moment when I thought 'what if she is pregnant?', it was actually quite scary. Like, I think I'd have a massive panic attack if I suddenly was a father, I'd have like somebody sitting there and I'd be responsible for it! I'd be like woah...I'd need a lot of Valium to get over it.

He commented that he would need to take Valium to cope with and recover from such an event. His use of this turn of phrase shows that again, he situated himself within a biological – as well as therapeutic – discourse here. Whether or not he would take it in a real situation – as doing so would be to oppose the naturalness discourse discussed in the previous chapter – the fact that he considers a drug as a mode of recovery suggests that such a feeling of anxiety is again, something considered as biological. Making sense of feelings of anxiety via the idea of a panic attack is also an interesting one; the panic attack features in the fourth edition of Diagnostic and Statistical Manual of Mental Disorders, published by American Psychiatric Association along with a host of physiological causes and symptoms, and so this again instantly renders the experience of negative emotions – whether panic or depression – as a somewhat biological or medical 'problem' or 'illness'. Thus, in both of these cases, people position themselves within not just a *therapeutic* discourse (via the use of emotional and introspective language) but also a *biological* discourse in the description of life events.

People, then, situate themselves within therapeutic discourse not only when giving accounts of happiness, but also when giving accounts of *un*happiness. Simultaneously, they also position themselves within the biological discourse in making sense of happiness and unhappiness as bodily, corporeal and internal processes. Emotional and introspective language, as well as a conception of unhappiness and negative emotions as something biological and internal, is therefore a central feature of the dominant discourses that people replay when producing accounts of their happiness and unhappiness.

Therapeutic reflections on the interview experience

Denise and Laurence both used therapeutic or introspective language to reflect on their experiences of being interviewed:

> *LH: Is there anything else you'd like to add before I switch the tape off?*
> Denise (46, female): No...I mean, that was interesting. I wasn't sure how and what direction that was going to go in, but no, that's...I'll be thinking about this later today! Not that I'd necessarily change answers, but just...sometimes you find yourself saying things and you don't realise...you hadn't previously sort of put that whole thought together, and you might suddenly think 'ooh, yeah, I suppose I do think that and I hadn't realised that!'.

> Laurence (65, male): There's a lot of ignorant people out there, and you've just got to be very wary. Like, I figured that you must have been very gay-friendly otherwise you wouldn't have been in this position. If it had been an ordinary club and you'd said can I ask you questions about being happy, and it was a normal – well, whatever normal is – club, I'd have been more nervous thinking 'am I gonna give myself away here and see what her reaction is, because she doesn't know what I am?' You might have been anti-gay and could have given me a bad time, and I'd be getting very angry. I may have been on edge about it and felt nervous, and the answers might not have come out as freely as they have done. But you've been good, you've said your mm's in the right places!!

Denise talked about the way in which she planned on reflecting further on her experience later on that day, and that being interviewed had helped her to come to terms with some of her thoughts and ideas. Thus, it could be said that the interview in and of itself constituted a technology of the self, whereby she engaged in further 'work' on herself, and that further reflection increased her self-knowledge.

Laurence also gave an account of his reflections on the interview process, particularly with regard to my perceptions – as an interviewer – of him; he expressed anxiety that he had felt regarding the degree to which I would be accepting of his sexuality after recruiting him from a lesbian, gay, bisexual and transgender (LGBT) social group of which he is a member. Thus, the interview experience had also prompted him to reflect in some way on himself and his selfhood – knowledge that I as an interviewer was not 'anti-gay' and therefore accepting of his identity provided him with a sense of reinforced confidence, thus again, giving rise to an increased self-knowledge for Laurence. Therefore, even when talking about their interview experiences themselves, it can be seen that some respondents situated themselves within therapeutic discourse – and may have even gained happiness – when making sense of this.

Conclusion

This chapter has illustrated the way in which people situate themselves within therapeutic discourse when making sense of their experiences of happiness and, indeed, unhappiness. Thus, when doing so, happiness is conceived of in a number of ways concerning the self, many of which are also central to self-help narratives. That is, it is considered to be something that is experienced at the level of the individual: a personal and subjective experience that is psychological in nature and takes place at the level of consciousness. 'Working' on oneself, or self-care, is also considered necessary for the achievement or the experience of happiness, that is, to have *control* over one's life and inner thoughts and to strive to achieve personal 'goals'. To be happy also requires self-knowledge, often in the form of self-confidence and knowledge of where one's life is 'going'. In the cases of both working on and knowing oneself, the self is considered as something ontologically separate, with which one can have a relationship (Hazleden, 2003); it is the cultivation of a positive or 'healthy' relationship with one's self which is the foundation upon which such a discourse of happiness rests. *Un*happiness is also articulated via therapeutic discourse. Adverse events that occur in everyday life are described using introspective, emotional language, using vocabulary taken from the 'psy' disciplines and words such as 'trauma' and 'suffering', and it is in this way that such negative experiences (and the emotions that accompany them) are *medicalised* – that is, they are thought of in biological terms and rendered a physiological 'problem'. In other words, many people simultaneously replay two dominant discourses – therapeutic and biological – when talking about their experiences and perceptions of happiness.

Thus, by understanding happiness through therapeutic discourse, it can be shown how the permeation of culture and language from the 'psy' sciences and the self-help industry into realms of everyday life has led to the existence and provision of a modern linguistic framework with which many people make sense of their experiences of happiness. It is in this way that people replay dominant discourses – particularly therapeutic discourse, but also that of the biological – in producing their accounts of their experiences and perceptions of happiness.

Therapeutic discourse is clearly a fundamental way in which people in Britain – and in other Western cultures – can understand happiness, and it is such a discourse and linguistic framework – often combined with other discourses explored in this book – that goes some way to allow us to understand the modern conception of happiness to which people so often subscribe.

5
'Pack Animals'? Interpersonal Relationships and Happiness

Relationships with others (whether social, familial, intimate or sexual) could be said to have a major impact upon people's experiences and perceptions of happiness; indeed, 'family relationships' and 'community and friends' were two of the 'most important' 'Big Seven' causes of happiness identified by Richard Layard (2011), and social ties, or 'social capital', has been found to be linked to well-being more generally (Helliwell, 2003, Helliwell and Putnam, 2004). All of the people whom I interviewed spoke in some way about the importance of this, and therefore the assertion that this is an important determinant of happiness may well be applicable. As Chris (46, male) pointed out, 'we're pack animals...that's why personally, in my life I've worked hard at having close relationships with people'

Nevertheless, this association may not be as straightforward as some suggest. The idea that interpersonal relationships should play a major role in one's experience of happiness suggests an interesting contrast with the therapeutic discourse explored in the previous chapter, within which people situated themselves when making sense of happiness as something individual, internal and self-orientated. Could it thus be argued that the Western construction of happiness sits at the intersection between social or communitarian discourses (whereby emphasis is placed on the importance of friendship, community and belonging) and that of the individual or therapeutic? What is the relationship between these two seemingly disparate discourses? How might people organise their experiences and perceptions through each of them? This chapter will attempt to address these questions through an examination of people's accounts of the role of interpersonal relationships with others in their experiences of happiness, and then it will consider the ways in which such relationships might play a fundamental part in the social construction of happiness in contemporary Western societies.

The chapter will begin with a consideration of the extent to which the happiness of society is important for the happiness of individuals; that is, do people feel happy when they know that others around them – or, the rest of society – are happy? And furthermore, do they do so whilst also making sense of happiness as something individual, personal and subjective? It will then examine the importance of interpersonal relationships in people's lives in a general sense, and their relationship with happiness. Next, it will go on to explore the way in which people make sense of happiness in relation to love and sexual relationships, as these were two types of relationships that a large number of respondents described as being important for happiness. Similarly, a lack of such relationships was identified by some as a cause of *un*happiness, and it will thus go on to consider the ways in which people negotiate the absence of these relationships through the ideas of loneliness and singleness, before ending with a more general discussion of the ways in which discourses around interpersonal relationships compete or stand in tension with therapeutic discourse in accounts of happiness, as well as their significance for its social construction.

Happy society, happy selves?

If ties with others can be considered an important factor in people's experiences of happiness, one might expect that individuals would gain such a feeling from the knowledge that the world or the society they live in is a 'happy' place. Indeed, a small number of respondents expressed this idea, like Chris, who felt that one is happy when there is a 'happy world':

> *LH: What do you think happiness actually is?*
> Chris (46, male): Well, again, I think for me personally, it's often clouded by the idea of what I think happiness is for other people, because quite often, what makes me happy is what makes other people happy. I think you're happy when there's a happy world.

It's hard to be happy and then walk outside and go 'oh my god, this is all horrid'.

In explaining what he thought that happiness is, Chris situated himself in a discourse that runs counter to that of the therapeutic; for him, his happiness was determined by the happiness of others rather than by any individual or internal processes. However, he expressed this by describing his own personal happiness as something distinct from – or something that is 'clouded' by – the happiness of others. This suggests that he nevertheless considers happiness to be something that is experienced at the level of the individual self, and includes a therapeutic dimension. Eileen similarly talked about the way in which the sight of suffering in other parts of the world was, for her, a major source of unhappiness:

> Eileen (63, female): ... I always say if you've got your health you can be happy. But going back to what I said before, if you see a young parent with a child disabled, in a wheelchair, how can those parents be totally happy, inside? Because it's heartbreaking... heartbreaking, really. And you see how other kids in the world, how in underprivileged, third world... how those children... I've never been out there, it's something I'd like to do actually, I'd like to go out and help those underprivileged... I know a woman who's doing that at the moment, she's older than me. And to see those kids at the school that they built out there... they'd never had anything. But now these children have been nourished, and have an education, they're happier, you see. So if, like me, you've seen suffering, it makes me unhappy, when I see suffering.

Again, Eileen's account contrasts with therapeutic narratives of happiness as she describes the way in which images of human suffering in other parts of the world (that is, something that exists outside of her individual self) bring about a feeling of *un*happiness. However, as with Chris, her account also suggests that she may consider happiness to be an individual, internal experience, as she speculates about the 'inner' happiness of parents of disabled children, thus also resonating in part with therapeutic discourse. Gillian also gave an account in which she described the way in which her understanding of capitalism in society made her feel unhappy:

> Gillian (46, female): ...a few years ago, I didn't work for a while, I actually didn't work for four years, by choice. But in that time, I did lots and lots of reading, different things, stuff on the Internet, books that people had lent me...And I remember getting very depressed, I kind of think I had a bit of a meltdown. And what it was...I had more time to think, and more time to read, and when I realised how the world works, especially how capitalism works, and how from our actions, what's happening on the other side of the world, it kept crashing down on me, and I was just...that made me really unhappy. But you come through it a stronger person, 'cos you kind of realise, you know, how the system is set up and it's not really for working people, it's for big business. And you know, when you put this out to people, they go 'oh, well that's just the way it is'...So that made me depressed, politics and world situations. [...] But, my philosophy is, you don't go round with your blinkers on, you learn about it, you know about it, and then you've got to find the joie de vivre, what makes you happy to kind of lift yourself out of that, get over it.

In one sense, what Gillian has said – like that of Chris and Eileen – runs counter to the therapeutic discourse of happiness as she attributes some of her unhappiness to a system that exists at the level of society (that is, capitalism). She feels unhappy about the idea that capitalism does not benefit the majority of the population (working people like her). However, her account also *resonates* with the therapeutic discourse when she emphasises that coming to such a realisation has turned her into 'a stronger person'. That is to say, having an understanding of capitalism has helped Gillian to increase her self-knowledge and to therefore cultivate a better relationship with her self. She also stressed the importance of finding happiness when living in such a society, in order that one is able to 'lift oneself out' of negative thoughts. Thus, unhappiness that is caused by a macro-level process like capitalism may still be dealt with via some kind of technology of the self or individual-level understanding. Gillian has expressed this by situating herself in both communitarian and therapeutic discourses; many other respondents also drew upon both discourses in tandem, particularly when reflecting upon their interpersonal relationships. This will be shown and explored further later in the chapter.

The interesting thing about these three accounts is that Chris, Eileen and Gillian were the only three interviewees to attribute any of their happiness or unhappiness to such society-level concerns; the 'sociality' described by all other interviewees – as will be shown in the remainder of this chapter – was centred mainly around that of friends, family and immediate social networks. Thus, it could be said that whilst relationships with others play a major role in people's experiences of happiness, it may specifically be membership of a *personal community* of friends, relatives or colleagues, which is individuated and self-selected in nature (see Pahl, 2005, Wellman, 1979) that has a more prominent influence upon the contemporary construction of happiness in late modernity than more worldly or global issues such as capitalism and Third-World poverty. If this is the case more widely, then this is likely to pose considerable implications for the work that has been and is being done on happiness and well-being by the British national government. Policies that are developed and implemented in light of this work would need to consider personal communities and individual factors alongside society-level concerns. Indeed, the idea that local governments could concern themselves with strengthening relationships and communities has been suggested in the media, though not actually taken up (Carr-West, 2014). Such implications are considered in more detail in this book's final chapter.

The importance of social relationships

Every individual whom I interviewed talked in some way about the way in which their interpersonal relationships with family and friends played a role in their experiences of happiness (or indeed, unhappiness); for example, this was the case for Maureen, Gillian and Linda:

> LH: *What would you say makes you most happy in life?*
> Maureen (80, female): That my children are well, and my husband is well, that is the most important thing in my life. My family, that they keep well. That's the most important thing. Family

is most important. Health…in the family…health, and their happiness.

LH: *Why do you think that having money and material things doesn't make us that happy?*

Gillian (46, female): …because I think it's relationships that really make you happy…I mean, it's nice to have nice food, and when you get paid you go out and you buy certain things, so…I just think we live now too much in a consumer society, and people's expectations are higher. […] But I'd say it's experiences, good experiences that make you happy and I think it's actually people that make the experiences.

Linda (65, female): …family things [have made me happy]. I mean, the day…both my children, the day they got married, they were very happy days in my life. The day my first grand-child was born was a very happy day. Although it was stressful at the beginning [laughs]. It ended up a very happy day! I look back on days…when I've had a really enjoyable day out with friends or something like that, or a really enjoyable holiday, you know. And I look back on days when my children were little and we did things…had family days out or something…you know, just little things that you remember.

The individuals giving each of these three accounts express that for them, relationships and experiences with family and friends are of high importance for the experience of happiness. In a similar vein, other respondents talked about how a *lack* of interpersonal relation-ships may be likely – either for themselves or for others – to induce a feeling of *un*happiness:

Tom (25, male): I was talking to an ex-girlfriend of mine last week, and she's earning a good amount of money and she's done loads of travelling, and she's already got a couple of holidays booked for this year, some really great ones, but she said she was unhappy. How can you be unhappy? You've got the things I want, you've got the interesting job, with responsibility, you get paid decent money, you know, go on holidays…why would she be unhappy? Well…I know that she hasn't got as many friends, or her personal life isn't going well, she hasn't got anyone to talk to, she hasn't really got any close friends around, she's lost quite a few friends through moving away or whatever...so it's all relative I think.

Tom described his ex-girlfriend's life and expressed surprise at her admission that she felt unhappy; he speculated that a good job, income and holiday prospects are all factors that *should* make a person happy. However, he also recognised that the real source of her unhappiness was a lack of close friends, thus suggesting that this is something that is likely to lead to unhappiness, even in seemingly favourable additional circumstances such as a good income and gainful employment. Beth also talked about how she might feel in a hypothetical situation in which she had no friends or family:

> *LH: Do you think we need to have good relationships with friends and family in order to be happy?*
>
> Beth (23, female): ...I feel like I do...I mean, I've had this conversation before, where I've thought to myself, if something really terrible happened, like, god forbid, all your family and all your friends die, I'd like to believe that you'd be able to pick yourself up and continue. But then, I think you'd have to make new friends...and new family. So yeah, I guess so. I think people are important...I think if I lived on an island all by myself, I wouldn't be that happy. Because I think that's what life's about, ultimately...you know, caring about people and having people care about you.
>
> *LH: Do you think people with no friends or family could be happy?*
>
> Beth (23, female): I think it would take a special kind of person. Erm, but probably. I don't know, it's one of those things where you think on the surface, they might be really happy but then maybe deep down...erm...for somebody like me it would be impossible. I just don't see the point in living, if it's just you. I'd be alright if it was just a short-term thing, but if it was forever... no. There's nobody to share anything with. Yeah, I wouldn't like it at all. I could live by myself, but I'd have to have people to visit, or...Yeah. I think there's a lot of sad people that are living on their own for whatever reason...I do think they are sad. I don't think there are many people out there who are all by themselves that are happy. Well obviously if they're not completely sane, or something...[laughs], but not with a sane

mind and everything else. Yeah, I think people are the essence of it all. Or even animals, maybe. But it's still like a living thing… to share things with.

She said that she would be unable to 'see the point in living' if she had no family or friends, and felt that people who live alone would be certain to feel unhappy about this; anyone in this position who did not would be likely to be mentally unstable, or lacking a 'sane mind', which suggests that the cultivation of relationships with others can be considered as a 'normal' or 'natural' route to gaining happiness. This can thus also be linked to the naturalness and biological discourses of happiness explored in the chapter 'What Is Happiness?' (Chapter 3), as it is assumed that the experience of happiness is a 'normal' part of one's mental and cerebral functioning. Danielle also gave an account that implied the normalcy of gaining happiness from relationships, when describing her brother's life:

> LH: *Do you think that good relationships with friends and family are important?*
> Danielle (26, female): I think to most people they are. Obviously, some people are different and they don't feel such need to have other people and they can feel perfectly happy… without all that. But I think to the vast majority of people, having good relationships helps you be happy. For instance, my brother is very odd. He seems very happy from day to day… but he's twenty-four and he's a student, lives at home still, and… he really only has one good friend who he'll see maybe once a week or so, and then apart from that, he just goes into uni, comes straight home, doesn't socialise with his uni friends, and then he'll just sit and laugh and joke with my mum and dad [laughs]. And he seems to be perfectly happy doing that! […] I mean, if I had that existence, I'd be pulling my hair out!

She described her brother as 'odd' because he does not have very many friends but nevertheless appears to be happy; she imagined that for herself, being in that situation would lead to unhappiness. Again, like with Beth's account, this suggests a normative dimension to the forming of relationships; that is, it is considered normal or natural to seek happiness through relationships with friends, and any individual who does not conform to this may be considered 'abnormal' by others. Although Danielle situated herself within therapeutic discourse at other points in her interview when reflecting upon her own happiness, she did not do so here; that is, she did not consider the possibility that her brother's happiness may come from within his own self, but rather assumed that gaining happiness from relationships with others was the norm.

Many people – when reflecting upon the *reasons* for why such relationships are an important part of a happy life – described the way in which they are a necessary source of *support* in helping them to get through their everyday lives. Thus, despite situating themselves within therapeutic discourse and making sense of happiness as something individual and internal (which can be seen in the previous chapter), they nevertheless emphasised that the provision of social and emotional support from family and friends was a major source of happiness. Chloe and Martin both talked about this:

Chloe (26, female): I think friends are important, but family is just that foundation, that absolute support network that you bounce off, that I think underlies most of my happiness...I think it underlies most of my confidence that therefore gives me happiness. 'Cos I know that whatever I do, I've got people going 'yeah, yeah, that's a great idea, you're amazing.' [laughs] And they're blood, and they also have that constant 'I'm never going anywhere'...which is, in terms of the unhappiness that may come from isolation or loneliness...I think knowing that there is a group of people that whatever happens, are always going to be there, and have stated that a lot, is invaluable.

Martin (32, male): ...around Christmas my girlfriend said that she needed to go back to New York, because she'd studied for three years already for her politics degree, she had to do her fourth year but she'd already taken two years out, so she had to go back. But for me it was so very difficult to accept. Because she'd sort of been my rock in many ways...You know, during my job search she was there for me...and during the burglary, her mum lives nearby, she could have gone and slept there where she felt safer but she stayed with me. I would never have been able to stay in that flat by myself, it was an old Victorian flat with a lot of windows...I would have thought I was stronger but I was scared shitless most of the time. So yeah, and then she was leaving me and I felt like my rock was taken away. And that's why I've felt that the last few months have been really shit.

Chloe described the happiness that she has gained from knowing that her family are there to support her, highlighting specifically that this is a safeguard against any isolation and loneliness which she may feel in their absence, and which would be a source of unhappiness. She also – by positioning herself within therapeutic discourse – expressed that she felt able to use their support as an aid to increasing her confidence, and thus, working on herself in order to do so, which would have enabled her to strengthen the positive relationship that she may have had with her self.

Martin talked about the way in which his girlfriend had offered him support during a number of adverse or difficult times in his life, such as a burglary and a period of unemployment. He attributed his unhappiness at the time of his interview to her absence (and thus, to the absence of her support). Many other respondents also identified a partner, close friend or family member as being their 'rock', or someone in whom they could confide, and talked about the way in which such support was necessary for being happy.

Thus, it appears that there is a discordance or tension between this emphasis on interpersonal relationships and the therapeutic discourse that has been shown to be so central to the construction of happiness. If happiness is something that can be gained from within oneself, by 'working' on oneself, then why are close relationships and the provision of emotional support that accompanies these perceived to be so fundamental for a happy life? And why are social networks considered so important in our supposedly individualised society? Might people draw upon the two discourses in tandem, in making sense of their experiences? The way in which relationships and social connections are considered so paramount may indeed take on a therapeutic dimension; this will be explored and these questions will be addressed throughout the rest of this chapter.

Being in love

Love and intimate relationships can, for many people, be a key source of happiness. Indeed, almost every individual who was interviewed talked about how these kinds of relationships (that is, relationships with partners) did – or could potentially – play an important part in their experiences of happiness. Martin, for instance, talked about the way in which his relationship with his girlfriend had made him feel happier:

> Martin (32, male): ... in some ways I've had more happiness than ever before, exactly because I have – for the first time in my life, like a steady relationship, you know. Two summers ago, I would have gone out and I would have met some girl in a club and dated her for a month and then broken up ... and it's not even really a relationship. But ever since I met my girlfriend, for the first time I had a feeling I'd met somebody who I could con- nect with. So, despite all of the difficulties there were in the last year, for example, I was burgled, I was in a way intensely happy. [...] When I was a student, I had a flatmate, she was twenty- three, and she had a boyfriend who was much older, forty-five, and she once said to me 'from a certain age, a man needs to be loved'. And I think there's a certain truth in that ... like, the fact that there's somebody there for you is a tremendous sort of ... support. So yeah, I think a good relationship is something that can make you happy.

For Martin, this kind of a relationship – in which he felt that he connected with someone on an emotional level – made him happier than his previous, short-term relationships with women, which were largely of a sexual nature. It was this added dimension of emotional connection and support that he felt was contributing to his happi- ness, which he was also able to maintain despite some adverse events that he had recently experienced.

The status of love and intimate relationships is also elevated for many people; some described the feeling they draw from them as 'better than' or 'exceeding' happiness:

> LH: *Do you think that being in or falling in love is important for being happy?*
> Denise (46, female): Oh, this week I'd say yes! [laughs] Yeah, I mean, I don't think it's the only thing, and I think you can be happy if you're on your own. But ... it's better if you are. It's a dif- ferent happiness. Yeah ... it's better, it's better. I don't know how

I'd define that. But it is more than just happiness. Oh, I feel like I'm twelve again! [squeals and laughs]

LH: In what way is it better?

Denise (46, female): I don't know...it is the sharing...my son is a large part of what makes me happy, but he needs to go and do his own thing, and I think we'll pretty much always have a good relationship, but...that's one sort of love, that's one sort of closeness. [...] I mean, a relationship where we are essentially equals, but sometimes he will need more support from me, sometimes I will need more support from him, and it can sort of veer between the two. Being in a relationship, I don't have to think 'ooh, I shouldn't tell you this, I need to find a different friend', being able to share pretty much any and everything with that one person...that's all the boxes ticked. And pleasing on the eye! [laughs]. Six foot three...

Denise described being in love as being 'more than just happiness' and identified the ability to *share* her life with her partner as the main reason for this. Describing love in this way, whereby she described feeling like a child or teenager again after having met someone new (and thus, alluding to an 'imagined', other world), is linked to the way in which 'being in love in some way places the lover outside the mundane, everyday world' (Jackson, 1993:211). Indeed, Roland Barthes describes this state as 'disreality' (Barthes, 1978). Many other respondents also highlighted the ideas of sharing and connection as a fundamental part of relationships. However, the idea that sharing should make a person happy – or indeed, more than just happy – again, runs counter to the way in which the self is constructed via therapeutic discourse as an autonomous individual who is able to 'work on' or develop a relationship with itself, and it is doing so that can then induce a feeling of happiness. At the heart of this narrative is the idea that one ought to only find such happiness from within their self. Thus, why might people also identify love and the sharing of their life with another person as one of the biggest sources of happiness? Do these two traditions of thought relate to one another in any way? How might individuals negotiate and make sense of their relationships with both their selves and with others? These questions will be raised again and addressed fully later in this chapter.

The feeling of being in love as being 'complete' or 'as one' also runs counter to the therapeutic tradition:

LH: Why did [being in love] make you feel so happy?

Chris (46, male): Because it was the start of stuff, I mean, it was the start of something...there was a lot of newness that was attached to that, there was a lot of...the concept of commitment was really there, erm, the sense of being very complete, in the sense of I think the minute you have children, there's a sense of completeness that comes in when they're very young, and your relationship is very young...you know, nothing's fucked up yet. So it's like, it's all pretty good. You've got a blank slate, it's tabula rasa for both. It was like, lord knows where this is gonna go, but I'm enjoying it. [...] I think falling out of love is the most miserable, miserable state that a person can be in, personally.

LH: In what way do you think sexual relationships are important for being happy?

Eileen (63, female): [...] I think it's just...the sexual relationship is an important part of being close to one another. And it makes you happy. I think it does anyway. It just makes you realise that you are sort of...as one, if you like. Like two halves of a whole. That is why, when people lose their partner, it's like half of them goes. It is quite true, it does. I don't go out anymore in the evenings because Keith's not with me. I don't like being at a party...I mean, I have to be at parties with the family and things like that, and friends...but I don't like it. Because Keith's not there. [...] I lost my confidence totally when Keith died, and I cannot...it just feels like it will never be the same again, for me to go out in a group or to a party. It will never be the same again. So I prefer not to go, to be honest.

For Chris, being in the early stages of a loving relationship made him feel 'complete'; this was particularly applicable to the start of a relationship, before problems begin to arise, and suggests that to be alone, one's self would be incomplete. He also felt that the end of such a relationship could be the largest potential source of unhappiness for people. Eileen's account, although in relation to sex, could also be applied to love. She similarly described the way in which one can feel like they and their partner are 'as one'. It is in this way that the self or subjectivity can be constructed through the dominant idea of love as 'complete' (or indeed, 'incomplete' if one is not in love) (Johnson, 2005:87). In talking about the death of her partner four years previously, she used the language of 'completeness' or 'wholeness', by describing feelings of loss of confidence, and of one half of herself. The idea that another person can make an individual feel 'complete' or 'whole' suggests that without that person, the individual or the self is incomplete in some way. In Eileen's case, positioning herself in this dominant discourse of love and 'completeness' leads to the idea that she does not consider herself as an autonomous individual who 'knows' herself; rather, she feels that she lacks self-knowledge – and also lacks confidence – because her partner (or a part of her) is no longer there. Thus, on the one hand, the fact that Eileen's relationship with her partner helped her to feel like a 'complete' person suggests that she is positioning herself in a discourse that places relationships as paramount, opposing that of the therapeutic. On the other hand however, she talked about herself and her partner within the therapeutic discourse, as though they were *one self*. She expressed unhappiness at her loss of confidence brought about by her partner's death, and implied that happiness could be regained if only she were able to reinstate a sense of self-knowledge and a good relationship with herself *as one individual*, rather than two, in order to thus feel complete again. Therefore, two contradictory discourses have been drawn upon in giving this account of loss.

Beth also situated herself in both discourses, by giving a rather contradictory account of her ideas about love:

> *LH*: *Do you think being in or falling in love is important for feeling happy?*
> Beth (23, female): I think that…really I think that happiness comes from the inside. I think ultimately, you have to make yourself happy, I don't think a relationship can make you happy. It's like superficial happiness I think. But…I like being in a relationship, but a good one. But I'm trying to keep my head screwed on, and saying that isn't the be all and end all. But as long as you have people around you, that do love you, be it friends, be it a relationship…yeah, it'd be alright.
> *LH*: *Have you ever been in love?*
> Beth (23, female): I have! [laughs]

LH: Did it make you happy?

Beth (23, female): Yeah it made me happy, but it's just the same way as friends make you happy... being loved, loving somebody, laughing together. Yeah, just... having somebody to share things with, and someone that knows you so well as well. You bounce off each other and understand each other, I guess. You felt safe as well. Yeah, safe... it makes bad things go away. You know, say you're worried about work, or something like that, you've got somebody who's just gonna... take it away.

She started her account by emphasising that it is not possible to gain happiness from a relationship, as happiness comes from the individual as opposed to anything external, thus drawing upon therapeutic discourse, in outlining the importance of self-sufficiency (Hazleden, 2003). However, she then talked about the way in which previous relationships did make her happy; like for Denise, it was the sharing aspect of these that were the reason for this. Thus here, she then goes on to position herself within a discourse that emphasises the importance of relationships. Again then, this raises a question: why has she contradicted herself in such a way? It is unlikely that Beth is simply forgetful or fickle, as these contradictions were manifest in the accounts of happiness of a large number of interviewees. A question can therefore be raised: if it is assumed that happiness comes 'from the inside', what role would a loving relationship play in the experience of happiness?

A diminished need to think about oneself was highlighted by some as a reason for why they draw happiness from intimate relationships. As Nick commented:

Nick (25, male): I think people look for meaning to their lives, so if they find someone... Also as well, we're in an age where we're too self-obsessed, we're encouraged to be self-obsessed, we're encouraged to be self-sufficient, you know, we're in the age of cocaine and caffeine, and fast cities and overcrowding, and that puts this fast thing into everyone, so to have someone to care about, to take your mind's eye off yourself, is quite comforting. 'Cos suddenly to have someone to care more about than yourself, makes you feel good about yourself, the fact that you can do that in the first place. Like you go wow, you're amazing, and suddenly you're thinking about them, and you want them to be happy rather than constantly worrying about am I happy, am I happy.

Again, this account suggests opposition to therapeutic discourse; rather than focusing upon the way in which happiness can be found from within oneself, Nick highlighted the way in which happiness can be gained from the idea that one is able to devote their attention to someone *other* than oneself, thus resonating with the relationships discourse within which many people have been seen to situate themselves. Indeed, Nick's conception of having a partner is intimately bound up with social factors here, as he links it with wider social changes and a rapidly changing environment. His account, then, echoes Beck and Beck-Gernsheim's suggestion that love and intimate relationships are sought as a response to modern social fragmentation. They write that 'individualization may drive men and women apart, but paradoxically it also pushes them into one another's arms. *As traditions become diluted, the attractions of a close relationship grow*' (1995:33, italics in original). However, as with some of the other accounts presented in this chapter so far, it could be said that therapeutic discourse has also manifested itself here. Whilst Nick talked about the way in which caring for others is a source of happiness, he did so by expressing that 'it makes you feel good about yourself', or that it allows for the individual to 'work' on themselves and to maximise or further their self-knowledge. He also equates finding a partner with the search for 'meaning' for one's life, which, again, is another therapeutic precept. Thus whilst the *source* of happiness can be made sense of from within a discourse of relationships (where the source is relationships with others), people may nevertheless come to terms with the actual *experience* of happiness by offering an account of it from within a therapeutic discourse.

Overall, then, love and intimate relationships are things considered by most to be positive and associated with happiness (or indeed, something 'more' than this, a 'disreality' (Barthes, 1978)). However, a contradiction has started to emerge: if happiness is constructed in the contemporary West as something individual, internal and self-orientated, then why do people also emphasise the centrality of social networks and interpersonal relationships to their experiences of happiness? Whilst most people make sense of love and relationships by positioning themselves in a discourse whereby happiness is gained directly from the connections and the sharing with another individual, some do so by constructing a narrative that stems from both this *and* the therapeutic discourse. That is to say, that whilst it is acknowledged that connections with others are a *source* of happiness, people situate themselves within more of a therapeutic discourse when making sense of their actual experiences of happiness, by explaining it as a process that takes place at the level of the individual self, where self-knowledge can be furthered and maximised. Why is it that these two seemingly disparate discourses are being employed in tandem here? If interpersonal relationships are considered so paramount for a happy life, how have individualisation, autonomy and freedom become so highly valued in the contemporary West? These questions are addressed in detail at the end of this chapter.

The next two sections of the chapter will further explore the way in which these two discourses are combined in the creation of accounts of happiness, through the themes of sexual relationships and the way in which people deal with both singleness and loneliness.

Sexual relationships

Sexual relationships have also been identified as a major source of happiness. When asked whether they felt that they were an important aspect of a happy life, many interviewees felt that they indeed were, as they involved the satisfaction of a 'natural' desire (thus situating themselves within the naturalness discourse when doing so). Sexual attraction can be considered a 'natural', biological process (in the same way as happiness itself is) by people who position themselves within a biological discourse. Heterosexual sex is considered to be natural in this way because of the way in which conception and reproduction are seen to be natural and innate needs (Johnson, 2005).

A distinction was made by the vast majority of people between sex within an established intimate relationship and sex that takes place outside of such relationships (or 'casual' sex); they emphasised that the former type of sex is far more conducive to happiness than the latter. Mark, for instance, talked about his promiscuous past:

> LH: *Do you think that sexual relationships are an important aspect of a happy life?*

Mark (41, male): [long pause] They're not the be all and end all...
in balance, yes they can be a component. But then, when you
look at the gay scene as well, often it's like wham bam quick
shag and I'm sorry what did you say your name was again?
That's if you get their name in the first place. I suppose in many
respects...I mean, I'm forty-one, I'm a fairly typical gay man,
I've been, as I said, round the whole of Babylon, I've been very
promiscuous in my past...probably the men I've had sex with
counts to the thousands...[...] I got it completely out of balance, because I used sex as a...tool...for validation. If somebody
wanted me, if they wanted me sexually, they still wanted me,
therefore I must be a person of worth. And when you try that
five, six, seven, even eight times over a weekend, it's really...
it leaves you empty. This is actually where...I'm not shy of sex
these days, but I shy away from the casual anonymous encounters because I'm looking for something more special. And now
sex for me becomes better with somebody that I...know. So sex
is important.

Mark positioned himself in a dominant discourse around sex by
emphasising that sex would be more likely to make him happy if
it were to take place within an established relationship; he described
the feelings brought about by his past experiences of casual sex as
negative. Indeed, other respondents also used this discourse in this
way. This type of discourse around sex is dominant because it is
bound up with the ways in which sexual expression is regulated by
normative ideals of love (Johnson, 2005). Beverley Skeggs (1997) suggests that this discourse exists, and is used in order to legitimate
particular types of sexual expression, and it is heterosexuality that
has produced these. According to Skeggs, people – and in particular,
women – position themselves in such discourses in response to a normative expectation to be 'respectable' and to conform to an image of
legitimate heterosexuality.

In describing his past, Mark made sense of himself in relation to
his gay identity, and the happiness that he now hopes to achieve
from a long-term relationship is channelled by a desire to move away
from what he deems a 'typical' gay lifestyle. Thus, although he seeks
a long-term relationship with another man, by positioning himself in
this discourse of sex, he expresses a wish to move towards a lifestyle

that more closely resembles one of legitimate heterosexuality. He had hoped that his previous casual encounters would have helped to increase his self-worth, but instead it resulted in a feeling of *emptiness*. Thus, whilst highlighting a desire to be in a long-term relationship at present, he has also positioned himself within therapeutic discourse by making sense of the desired outcome of sex as that which would impact upon his sense of self and which would allow him to work on himself. The anonymous sexual encounters in which he took part in the past resulted in a loss of self-knowledge, thus rendering his relationship with his self weakened.

Like Mark, Sophie also asserted that casual sex is a potential source of unhappiness:

> LH: *What about casual sex, outside of relationships, do you think that can make people happy?*
> Sophie (22, female): I think it makes people unhappy. I think people who constantly have one night stands are obviously looking for something that they're not going to find from a one-night stand. Sometimes you'll meet someone, you'll get on, there'll be chemistry, you'll have a one-night stand, but it's like you're meant to be anyway. Well not always. But people who are serial one-night stand people, I think obviously something's missing in their lives and they're doing it to.... I don't know, as a way of... finding themselves somehow, and I don't think it makes them happy. You know, sometimes people want something meaningful, and they just never have had...

Although Sophie had not experienced casual sex herself, she speculated that those who have might expect to 'find themselves', or 'form a healthy relationship with the self' (Hazleden, 2003:421), as Mark indeed did. Her account implies that sex within a relationship would be more 'meaningful', and may be a more optimum route to 'finding' oneself, or increasing one's self-knowledge. Again, then, Sophie positioned herself within the same dominant discourse as Mark; as a heterosexual woman, she sought to conform to a model of 'respectability' and legitimate heterosexuality (Skeggs, 1997) in replaying this discourse. In doing so, she expressed the idea that sex should be equated with intimacy and love, and it is only when this is the case that sex is 'meaningful' (Johnson, 2005). It is this model of sexual expression that – according to this discourse – is most conducive to happiness.

Sophie, then, positioned herself within both a relationship-oriented discourse and therapeutic discourse in this account; she expressed at another point in her interview that she would like to be in a long-term relationship, but by making sense of sex as a means of self-expression (whereby one can 'find themselves'), she also situated herself within therapeutic discourse.

Lizzie also expressed the idea that sex which is equated with love is the form of sexual expression most conducive to happiness, and felt that any potential 'casual' sexual experiences would result in a loss of self-confidence:

> *LH*: *What is it about [one-night-stands] that wouldn't make you happy?*
> Lizzie (25, female): Well I think it would make me less confident in trying to find the person who I would really want to be with, and also I'd lose confidence in myself. I think that having relationships like that back to back...almost downplays how I think that men should be. If I am constantly meeting these people, these guys who only want to sleep with you once or sleep with you twice, after a while, I'd just get this image in my head that that's what all guys are like. And I don't think that's the way that I want to...portray the opposite sex. [...] Having a sexual relationship with someone you love is the most amazing thing, and so I don't think that...I mean I can't obviously say I'm perfect in all respects or anything, but I guess at the end of the day that's what I want, and so I think if I'm going to sleep around a lot, I think that would have a detrimental effect on my long-term goal.

Lizzie, again, replayed the dominant discourse of sex that is characterised by the association of sex and love, and said that she would lose confidence if she ever failed to conform to such a model of 'legitimate' heterosexual expression. Thus, she also situated herself within therapeutic discourse in this account; she described her perceptions of casual sex in terms of its detrimental impact upon her sense of self and on her ability to find the 'right' partner, which she considered to be a long-term goal and thus something that she was able to work at. Whilst she also felt that sex that takes place within a loving relationship was the form of sexual expression most conductive to happiness, for her it was also an act that was able to affect her confidence, self-perception and self-knowledge.

So for Mark, Lizzie and Sophie, sexual expression that is bound up with love is that which is most likely to lead to happiness. That is to say, that when positioning oneself within this dominant discourse of sex and happiness, happiness is most commonly brought about, produced or experienced in relation to a conformity to models of legitimate heterosexual expression (Johnson, 2005, Skeggs, 1997).

However, conforming to models of legitimate heterosexual expression is not the only discourse available to people when making sense of their feelings towards their sexual relationships. Casual sex can also be regarded positively, and not conducive to unhappiness:

> Martin (32, male): I went back to [home country] for four years and as a trainee in a law firm I didn't have any fun, I just worked, I didn't have many friends. I had a girlfriend once in a while but I don't think I'd really satisfied my ambitions as a man, in terms of women. So I came here, and yeah, went out so much and you can have tons of girlfriends, so you sort of feel like you compensate for what you feel you might have been missing. But yeah... maybe I overcompensated, as people often do. I remember one time, I even had two girlfriends at the same time, once in the summer, I woke up with one girl and I went to bed with another one in the evening. And in a way that made me feel good. Something now I wouldn't even have the strength for, or the desire. But back then, it did. And you know, maybe it's something you have to do as a man.

Martin's account here is clearly different to the three presented previously in terms of its positive aspect; however, there are also similarities. He highlighted the way in which sex as an activity brought him happiness – both casual sex, and sex with his long-term girlfriend, which he talked about at another point during his interview – and he thus situated himself within a discourse whereby relationships were favoured. Moreover, he also positioned himself within therapeutic discourse by making sense of casual sex as a means of the satisfaction of ambitions, of expression of his masculinity, and therefore of his self and identity. Thus again, through sex, Martin was able to work on himself and maximise his self-knowledge.

The idea that casual sex is inferior to sex within an established relationship appears to be the dominant discourse that people use with regard to sexual relationships; indeed, whilst Martin provided positive reflections upon casual sex, he was the only interviewee to do so. He did not express a wish to conform to a model of heterosexual feminine 'respectability', and instead, expressed his heterosexual masculinity. However, it may be the case that other respondents may also have felt this; indeed, as Lizzie and Sophie suggest, it is an activity that people do engage in. Nevertheless, there is a dominant discourse around sexual relationships that people may replay in an attempt to come across in a more 'respectable' light, particularly when divulging feelings and opinions about sex to an interviewer.

People's accounts of their perceptions of sexual relationships very much echoed that of the first three accounts presented here; largely, sex within established intimate relationships, and which was associated with love, was considered as more conducive to happiness than casual sex, as happiness here is inextricably bound up with a conformity to legitimate heterosexual expression. It was this normative discourse that most people were seen to replay. Further, each of the four accounts presented in this section (as well as many others that were given on this subject) assumed a particular relationship with and conception of the self; sex was conceived of not only in terms of a relationship with another individual (whether physical, intimate, emotional or all three) – and thus experiences of happiness were made sense of via a relationship-based discourse – but also via therapeutic discourse, in which it was considered a 'technology of the self' in which one was able to further their relationship with their self – or indeed weaken, in the case of casual sex for some people. Indeed, it was the emotional component of sex within established relationships (which casual sex is seen to lack) that enabled this relationship to be maximised; a lack of emotional connection led to the weakening of this relationship.

Absent relationships: Loneliness and singleness

As has been shown in previous sections of this chapter, therapeutic discourse is increasingly pervasive in people's accounts of their interpersonal relationships; whilst such relationships are central to their experiences of happiness, many make sense of these from an individualised, self-orientated perspective. Despite its pervasiveness, being alone – in cases of both *loneliness* and *singleness* – was talked about by many people as one of the biggest sources of unhappiness. For instance, Linda speculated that people who have few or no friends or family are likely to be less happy than those who do:

> *LH: Do you think one needs to have good relationships with friends and family to be happy?*
>
> Linda (65, female): Yes. Yes, I do. I think people I know that haven't got much family or haven't got many friends are more unhappy than people who do. I suppose family are always there, even if you're not getting on too well with them. Family are there whether you like it or not! Nothing changes that hard relationship that is your family, and you sort of get together really. I don't know, I'm just very lucky I think, with mine...I haven't got lots of family, but the ones I've got I'm really lucky with. And they're all easy to get on with. Friends...I don't know, maybe it's because I haven't got lots of family, I do have a lot of friends. And because I live on my own I have lots of friends, and so you know, I think that's quite important, yeah. And I think that makes you happy. [...] I need friends and people to talk to, but I don't think everyone's like that. I think some people are quite happy... just living their life without friends. You know, people who are recluses. I don't think I recognise their happiness, but I suspect they're happy in their own way. I think it depends on the personality.

Being with family and friends was a major source of happiness for Linda; she felt that having people around with whom she could talk was a necessity. Whilst she recognised that this may not be the case for everyone, she felt unable to understand how anybody with no social network could be happy. She situated herself in the naturalness discourse of happiness, by making sense of the happiness of recluses (by attributing this to a natural, fixed aspect of their personalities), but her account also illustrates the normative nature of sociality. Like with that of Danielle's account of her brother's life earlier in this chapter, her inability to understand how such people could be happy – again – suggests that the cultivation of relationships with others is considered a 'normal' route to gaining happiness.

Gillian also highlighted the way in which she feels that loneliness is a source of unhappiness for people, and felt lucky that the fact that she is a twin meant that she had never had to experience this:

> Gillian (46, female): I think being a twin, actually, has helped me, because when people talk about loneliness, I have to say, I don't know what it is, I've never been lonely. People say 'yeah, but you don't live together', but when you're a twin, it's hard to explain, it's like you've always got somebody there with you, you know? So that's something I've never had. Yeah, that's another thing, loneliness, especially in cities. That makes people very unhappy. [...] I felt terrible when someone told me that the old man who lived opposite my block had been dead in his flat for three weeks, and I thought oh my god, nobody around knew, how awful is that? You hear about these things... But I was working full-time, I was never around during the day, do you know what I mean, so I wasn't going to be the person calling on him, but it does make you feel a bit shitty afterwards, you just think god, you're living in a block with sixty people, and nobody realised he was dead, that's kind of... and then you start thinking 'oh my god, maybe I'll end up like that', you know!

She recognised that loneliness is an increasingly large problem in cities and illustrated this by expressing sympathy for her neighbour who had no family or friends who were able to visit him. However, Gillian's account also contains an interesting contradiction; on the one hand, she talks about how being a twin means that she feels as though she has 'always got somebody there', and this for her is a source of happiness. However, as can be seen from earlier points in this book, Gillian also makes sense of some of her experiences of happiness via therapeutic discourse; thus, despite the fact that she feels as though she is never alone, she nevertheless conceives of happiness via an individualised and self-orientated conception of everyday life. This once again raises a question: if relationships with others are so fundamental to the experience of happiness, why is it made sense of via such an individualised discourse?

Loneliness was also described as a source of unhappiness by Laurence, who talked about his solution to this problem:

LH: Do you feel happy about your life generally?

Laurence (65, male): I feel a lot more contented. If you'd asked me that question last year, I would have been completely different, my mum died, and there were things that led up to it...No, I'm beginning to feel more contented. A little bit lonely though, I don't like loneliness. But it's up to me to do that, I think at the age of sixty-five, I'm hoping I can let it pass me by. That's the reason I joined this club, it's given me a great deal of happiness. There's a lot of people there who have experienced what I've experienced. [...] And being accepted more, you know. You feel like you can go up there and you don't have to hedge about your bets because you don't need to worry about how they'll react when you say 'oh by the way, I'm gay.' 'Oh, are you?'. Then you feel threatened because that person doesn't know what to say. And then you think perhaps you should have kept your big mouth shut. But going to that club, you don't...that's one big barrier you've got over, you know, because everyone else there's in the same position as you are.

Laurence described the LGBT group of which he is a member, and the way in which he had gained happiness from meeting others who had had similar experiences to his through this. Joining the group had helped him to make new friends, but it also helped him to feel more accepted as a gay man; knowledge that others were in the same position and accepted his identity was, for him, a big source of happiness. His account thus again points to the perceived importance of both being part of a community and knowing that others have the same experiences as oneself. Once more then, the question can be raised: if loneliness is such a problem and a source of unhappiness (and ties with others seen to be able to remedy this), then why is happiness simultaneously conceived of in terms of an individual-level, internal process?

Like loneliness, being single – that is, not in an intimate relationship – has also been highlighted as a source of unhappiness.

Chris, for instance, expressed sympathy for people who had never experienced falling in love:

> Chris (46, male): I always feel sorry for people who haven't fallen in love. I can only judge it for myself...but to me, being in love, even if it's just for, I don't know, a couple of months, a year, it's worth it for the enjoyment I've got out of that, the contentment that I've got out of that...like that expression, better to have loved and lost than never to have loved at all. I think that's quite true, I do think it's quite true. Because the thing is, you're born alone and you die alone. So the idea that you can actually be concerned, and be invested in someone to the degree that being in love with someone – being truly in love with someone – is a huge cause for joy.

Indeed, Lizzie described the way in which being single makes her feel unhappy:

> Lizzie (25, female): I guess the only thing that gets me down is the relationship side of things. I feel as though...I've been single for a while, and trying to find somebody, I've just found that to be really quite a difficult, daunting task as well. I've got a couple of friends of mine who have recently got into relationships, they're really happy...and I don't see that almost...to make me sad, obviously! But the less time I get to spend with them, I kind of reflect back on the fact that because of that, I'm not in a relationship, you know.
>
> *LH: Do you think if you were in a relationship, or if you met somebody, you'd feel happier?*
>
> Lizzie (25, female): I think so. I mean, not saying anybody, you know! But someone who I'd really like to be with, definitely. I think there are so many couples out there that just look as though...I can almost see how happy they are in themselves, and being around the other person, because...either they've met their match, or they complement each other so well. That's also a kind of goal that I have in life...at some stage I do want to get married and have children. So I like to think that within the grand scheme of things, to have somebody there at the end of the day would make me more happy. [...]...just having somebody

there for even a physical or a sexual relationship as well, is really healthy. And obviously, someone that you love and that you have that intimacy with and that you can share things with and...you know, just having that moral support. That's a really important part of life.

For Lizzie, having an intimate relationship with another individual is *healthy*; in other words, she positions herself within the naturalness discourse by considering it 'normal' to be in a relationship and expects that this would be a route to gaining happiness, particularly as many of her friends have done so. This resonates with the literature on singleness – particularly amongst women – in which singleness has been shown to have a stigmatised, inferior status, whilst heterosexual couples occupy a more privileged position in Western heteronormative culture (Budgeon, 2008). Despite understanding that it is a connection with and support from another person that would bring about a feeling of happiness (and thus situating herself within a discourse of sociality), she recognises that people who *are* in relationships are each happy *in themselves* as individuals, which, again, suggests that she makes sense of the potential experience of happiness that she could gain from such a relationship via therapeutic discourse.

Mark, like Lizzie, also disliked being single and felt that his happiness depended upon his meeting 'Mr Right':

> LH: *What would you say makes you most happy in life?*
> Mark (41, male): Oh god...I think it's this unobtainable – or what feels to be unobtainable – happy relationship. I've been very unlucky, so my happiness is dependent on whether I've met somebody or not. And if it goes well, or not. I suppose I'm by and large content if there isn't anybody there, and then the happiness if somebody very special, then it kind of goes off the scale and then if it all goes horribly, horribly wrong, which it always does, the happiness comes crashing back down and then I have to struggle to get back up to the content level. So that's a big part of the happiness in my life. It's dependent on meeting Mr Right!
> LH: *What is it about having a good relationship that you think would make you happy?*

> Mark (41, male): I suppose I've had to work hard on interpersonal relationships, and on the gay scene particularly, it's very difficult anyway, at the best of times…and then my family background as well hasn't been the best. So it's just the ideal, I think it's that element of love and being loved, nurturing…feeling secure, providing security for somebody. It also helps if they're a big hunk! But yeah, it's that element of…the special. And even the mundane, and by mundane I mean the grocery shopping…or coming home from work and saying 'hey honey, how was your day?'.

Thus, for Mark, despite the fact that he finds interpersonal relationships difficult, his account nevertheless suggests that for him, they are necessary; he does not have good relationships with many members of his family, and therefore feels that he needs an intimate relationship with a partner, and the security that this would bring to compensate for this. He expresses this need by positioning himself within a discourse of romance; Wendy Langford comments that romantic love 'should be understood as a narrative which "seduces" individuals to invest emotionally in the "religion of love", through the promise that entry into an exclusive union will deliver them from their "spiritual" ills' (Langford, 1999:35–36). Thus, love, in this way, can be considered as something that has the potential to alleviate feelings of unhappiness.

For both Mark and Lizzie (as well as the for the vast majority of the other respondents who were single), the idea of being in love or in a relationship with another person, and the feelings and emotional security that accompany this, is considered to be very desirable, and being single is not a status from which it is considered that one can gain happiness. This is indeed likely to be the case in the general population, as we have already seen from sociological literature that being single is a stigmatised status (Budgeon, 2008); this can also be seen with the growing popularity of online dating sites and singles' events. So why are such feelings desired by so many people? Why do people need emotional connection, love and security? And if – according to therapeutic discourse – we are autonomous, self-reliant individuals who are able to take control over our experiences of happiness, then what kind of a role should interpersonal relationships play in such experiences? The following section will attempt to address these questions.

The key to happiness: Sociality or autonomy?

So whilst it is clear that interpersonal, intimate and sexual relationships are all an important part of people's experiences and
perceptions of happiness, a major tension is also evident in people's
accounts of these; on the one hand, it is considered as something
that is experienced by the individual. One possesses a certain degree
of personal autonomy, and they are able to manipulate and 'work'
on their self in order to control and monitor their experiences
of happiness. On the other hand, as can be seen in this chapter,
social networks and interpersonal relationships are seen to be equally
important aspects of such experiences; it is emotional connections
and relationships with others that are considered to be the ulti-
mate source of happiness. Why does such a contradiction exist? Why
should interpersonal relationships play such a crucial role in the
experience of happiness in our seemingly individualised, therapeutic
society?

It is clear that therapeutic culture is that which people have been
socialised into, as it is this dominant discourse within which most
situate themselves when making sense of their experiences of happiness. Indeed, much work has also been done on illustrating the
process of individualisation that Western society has witnessed in
recent decades (Bauman, 2001, Beck and Beck-Gernsheim, 2001,
Furedi, 2004). The self-help movement (that is, books that advise
their readers on self-improvement, as well as the 'psy' expertise that
surrounds it more generally) is one major aspect of therapeutic culture. The therapeutic discourse that is employed in self-help texts
and by these 'experts' is based upon the idea that self-examination
and confession are means by which 'truth' is obtained (Rimke, 2000).
These precepts are, therefore, self-orientated (as, indeed, is therapeutic discourse more generally). Because they are founded upon
the belief that 'truth' resides within the individual, the idea that
such self-examination is intimately bound up with something that
is inherently social and exists *outside* the self – that is, the political
programmes of advanced neoliberal democracies and the production
of selves who are 'effective' citizens (Rose, 1996) – seems remark-
ably discordant with this. Indeed, 'self-help "expertise" serves to
undermine collective formations and the essential interdependencies
of selves' (Rimke, 2000:70). In other words, aspects of therapeutic

discourse (namely, self-help expertise), which is one of the dominant discourses within which people position themselves when producing their accounts of happiness, serve to *obscure* the aspects of human existence that are interdependent, intersubjective and social (and which contribute to the oft-held conception of humans as 'pack animals'). This tension that appears to characterise people's accounts of happiness in relation to interpersonal relationships, then, may be a result of this process. People may indeed have a desire to forge connections and relationships with others and to be politically and socially engaged, but they do this against a backdrop of self-sufficiency and self-examination that are central tenets of therapeutic discourse. In relation to intimate relationships, for instance, romance is promoted as a 'haven' from personal ills (Langford, 1999), and people seek happiness through loving and sexual relationships, by conforming to models of legitimate sexual expression (Skeggs, 1997). However, they nevertheless make sense of this through a discourse in which the needs of the self are paramount.

Although therapeutic discourse is a dominant tradition of thought by which people understand happiness, it could be suggested that such an individualised culture may not necessarily be a purely *positive* thing. As Erich Fromm (1942) has postulated, freedom and autonomy are two of the most central and important values of contemporary social life. However, according to Fromm, these may pose a *burden* on individuals, whereby they may be met with feelings of isolation, powerlessness and insecurity. That is to say that whilst medieval social systems were organised in such a way that everybody knew their place in society, and thus offered stability and relative security, the advent of capitalism, Fromm argued, instilled a feeling of uncertainty as each individual's position depended purely upon their own personal effort. Furthermore, this is still the case in contemporary capitalist society as individuals – particularly in urban locales – are overwhelmed by their environment (see Simmel, 1903) and thus experience a feeling of powerlessness and aloneness. Individuals are not necessarily aware of these feelings as they go about their daily lives; indeed, the respondents whom I interviewed did not explicitly claim to have had such experiences. However, many did express a wish for security and a need for this from a loving relationship; they also expressed a sense of unhappiness with regard to singleness and loneliness, and thus it may be so that their desire and need for interpersonal relationships, and their association of these with happiness, is the means through which they seek to cope with these feelings of isolation.

Fromm suggests that one way in which they may deal with these problematic feelings is by seeking some kind of *guidance* in life. For some people, this is done through religion, a belief in God and in religious values. Others would rely on guidance and support from friends, relatives or partners; indeed, many people acknowledged this and data presented earlier in this chapter illustrate this. Furthermore, it could be argued that people's adoption of 'therapeutic' and self-help precepts via their use of therapeutic discourse is a means of feeling more 'guided', as this is a body of knowledge and ideas that can be drawn upon in order to make sense of and understand one's own identity and their life and experiences.

A mechanism of escape from these feelings that Fromm has identified is a striving for either *submission to* or *domination of* another individual or object; it could be argued that this is achieved via intimate relationships. Indeed, many respondents expressed that the happiness that they derived from intimate relationships largely stemmed from the sense of *security* that these offered (and the respondents who were single similarly talked about a desire of such security from hypothetical relationships), and thus it is these relationships that can act as a safeguard against feelings of isolation and powerlessness. Submitting to or dominating over another person is, for Fromm, a way of coping with such feelings because they are means by which one can alter their sense of self (1942). By submitting to another person, an individual attempts to *lose* his or her self, as he or she attempts to become part of a larger, more powerful being; by dominating over a person, the self is *strengthened*. The self may never be completely lost, as people maintain an acknowledgement of their relationships with it when drawing upon therapeutic discourse; nevertheless, by seeking to alter one's sense of self in an intimate relationship, one is able to regain the sense of security that they may otherwise lose in an individualised society. Furthermore, it is this need for the eradication of these negative feelings that is the source of the happiness that people gain from interpersonal (and intimate) relationships.

Thus, happiness may be derived from interpersonal relationships because these may be one possible route via which security can be gained in an otherwise insecure, uncertain and individualised world. However, it is this individualised world which lies at the foundation of the therapeutic culture that so many are socialised into and which is so widely drawn upon when making sense of one's experiences of happiness. Therefore, one can conclude that the construction of happiness in Western societies does indeed lie at the intersection between therapeutic discourse and that of sociality, and that the tension between these two discourses that has been evidenced and displayed throughout this chapter is fundamental; whilst happiness is ultimately considered to be an individual-level experience that is made sense of in terms of one's relationship with their self, interpersonal relationships nevertheless play a crucial role in this experience as they mediate one's relationship with their self and are a necessary safeguard against the insecurity and powerlessness that characterise individualised capitalist societies in the twenty-first century.

6
Orientations to Money, Working Life and Happiness

This chapter provides an analysis of the ways in which people perceive the relationship between money and wealth and their experiences of happiness, as well as the ways in which happiness (or indeed, unhappiness) is experienced in their working lives. Financial situation and work have been identified as key determinants of happiness in much of the scholarly literature on well-being (see Layard, 2011, for example), both in terms of employment status and income levels, but also in terms of people's reported job satisfaction. They are therefore pertinent issues to explore sociologically. A number of questions will be raised: how do people position themselves within particular discourses when giving accounts of such things, and which discourses are available to them? In what ways do they make sense of their selves when doing so? And more fundamentally, how might they use therapeutic discourse to produce these particular accounts and perceptions?

Although the primary purpose of this chapter is to explore the relationship between money, work and people's experiences and perceptions of happiness, it also highlights the *classed* nature of happiness. The way in which people articulate their ideas about happiness, money and work is socially patterned – they draw on culturally rooted narratives and discourses in making sense of them – but the patterns that emerged for the people who were interviewed were distinctly *middle class* (as the majority of them were from middle-class backgrounds). We could expect that people from other backgrounds may articulate their ideas using different narratives, though this would be material for another book.

This chapter will first consider people's perceptions of the relationship between money and happiness and, in particular, their reflections on whether money and wealth are important for a happy life. Many interviewees used the term 'materialism' in talking about this, which was a term they used to refer to a desire for money and material possessions, as well as an accompanying expectation that happiness would be gained from the accumulation of this. The term shall be used in this chapter to refer to this idea. The discourses within which people situate themselves in terms of their perceptions of the relationship between this and happiness will thus be explored. How might people produce their selves through their accounts and these discourses? And in what way does therapeutic culture 'frame' this self-production and the way in which certain types of selves may be accorded value? The *classed* nature of these accounts, as well as the production of middle-class selves will also be explored.

It will then go on to explore people's accounts of the happiness, as well as the *un*happiness that they associate with their working lives. People position themselves within particular discourses, namely *therapeutic* discourse when talking about work; this will be examined via analysis of their accounts of their feelings of personal *fulfilment* and *achievement*. They also draw upon their experiences of work in order to attempt to 'work' on their selves so as to self-actualise and generate self-knowledge. However, the cultural resources and practices with which this 'work' is performed are not necessarily accessible to all, but only to those occupying particular structural positions. The way in which such accounts of fulfilment are bound up with, and are expressions of, classed aesthetics (Bourdieu, 1986) will be explored, as will the way in which selves are produced through discourse around working life.

The chapter will start with an examination of people's accounts of their orientations to money and happiness.

Consumption: A problem?

Possessing high amounts of money is frequently understood as not being conducive to happiness. All of those who were interviewed talked in some way about the way in which having a lot of money can be a negative thing in life.

The idea that the consumption of material goods has a stronger presence in contemporary British or Western society than in any other place or at any other time-point was highlighted by some interviewees. Mark, for instance, compared Western cultures to that of the East:

> *LH: Do you think that the idea of happiness is different across cultures?*
> Mark (41, male): ...Yes, I think it is, actually. Western culture is very much consumer-driven, I think it's the worship of money, money will buy you happiness. Eastern cultures...not that I'm by any means an expert, but they are more spiritual, and happiness comes from within. Peace kind of thing. I think it's very different in different cultures.

Mark – like many other respondents – did not subscribe to the idea that 'money will buy you happiness' himself, and he talked about this at another point during his interview. However, he identified this as an overall view of much of the rest of society and juxtaposed this with the Eastern, more spiritual view, in which happiness is seen to come 'from within'. His quote thus suggests that happiness does not come 'from within' for most people in the West, as they would draw it from 'external', material goods. A paradox has therefore emerged: as illustrated in Chapter 4, many people situate themselves within therapeutic discourse when giving accounts of their experiences and perceptions of happiness. That is to say, happiness is considered to be a very individual experience, and many people do indeed express that it comes 'from within', despite the fact that all respondents came from Western cultural backgrounds. So why might people (including Mark himself) appear to be subscribing to such an 'Eastern' conception that Mark has identified?

It seems that a 'materialistic' outlook on life (that is, one whereby money and possessions are perceived as conducive to happiness) is at odds with 'therapeutic culture'. Whilst therapeutic culture promotes the idea of the individual drawing happiness from within him- or herself (like the 'Eastern' conception that Mark mentions), a 'materialistic' person would supposedly draw it from material goods that exist *outside* the self. It is thus in this vein that all respondents describe consumption in negative terms (which will be shown in more detail in this chapter); reliance upon factors external to the self for one's happiness would run counter to the precepts of therapeutic discourse, whereby the importance of self-sufficiency of the individual is upheld (Hazleden, 2003), as well as contradict the ancient Greek principle of needing a 'balanced' soul that is free of any interference from external or material factors (Plato, 380BC/1998). Thus, if it is therapeutic culture through which people produce their accounts of happiness, it could be argued that the expression of such a non-'materialist' view is very much in accordance with – and is furthermore an *aspect of* – therapeutic discourses of happiness.

This non-'materialist' view was widespread amongst those interviewed; many talked about the way in which material things may not bring about happiness. Chloe and Lizzie expressed this idea:

LH: *Do you think that amassing material goods can lead to increased happiness?*

Chloe (26, female): I don't think your happiness should come from external…motivations, or material goods, or people… I think they can, and you'll probably get happy for a bit, but if you rely on that, you can always come back down again. I think it should always be an internal sort of…steadiness, and motivation, because that will never go, that voice inside you will never go…whereas Manolo Blahniks will go out of season [laughs]. I mean, I'm saying this but if I go out tomorrow and buy a really cute All Saints jacket, I'd be really pleased. But I try and personally concentrate myself on having an inner happiness where the outside events are good and bad, because I know that's the thing that will always be there. And I know so many people who are incredibly…wealthy, and aren't happy, because of searching… always feeling that their worth is in outside things. I know people who are very wealthy and are happy, but I know that's because they've always been happy, when they were striving for it as well.

LH: *Do you think consumerism makes people happy?*

Lizzie (25, female): To some extent, yes…because I think that's just a general way of life. People spend so much time these days shopping, and being shown adverts on TV, and you get a lot of pressure into feeling…that these are the things that should make you feel happy. And it does, to some extent, it definitely works... we get so much advertising that we're often not even aware of to show you things... products, that will actually improve your happiness. And you're naturally going to feel that way, as if yeah, if I do get such and such, I'm going to feel better about my life. I think that generally does have a large impact on... I guess on the world that we live in, and our expectations of happiness.

LH: Would you say that's the case for you personally?

Lizzie (25, female): [laughs] Well I always like to think that I'm an exception to the rule! I don't... I spend maybe, in comparison to the people that I know, a lot less time buying new things, and a lot more time either... outdoors or travelling, or often at the gym and things like that. So that's what makes me happy. Then again, I can't deny the fact that I like a good bargain, or I like to find something that's a bit special...

Thus, for Chloe, her expression of a non-'materialistic' view is indeed very much interwoven with therapeutic discourse; she likens happiness to a 'voice inside you', whereby the body – once again – is likened to a 'container' for one's happiness (see Lupton, 1998) and suggests that this more individually-derived, cerebral and self-sufficient experience is a more 'reliable' means of gaining happiness (see Hazleden, 2003), rather than drawing upon 'external motivations' like material goods. Lizzie's account alludes less to therapeutic discourse; however, both she and Chloe highlight the way in which they deviate from the widespread view held by others whom they know that consumption can provide happiness. On the other hand, they both acknowledge that they – despite deviating from this view – derive pleasure from buying new things; this is a commonly expressed attitude, as 'shopping and all the associated activities [...] are generally represented, and indeed often experienced, as pleasurable, as enjoyable' (Smart, 2010:144). They therefore do this whilst simultaneously recognising a negative dimension of consumption, whereby it may bring about dissatisfaction and debt (Schwartz, 2005).

Another layer of complexity is thus added to the paradox highlighted above, by the fact that people (like Chloe and Lizzie) claimed that they were not 'materialistic'. If, as they said, so many other Westerners *are* so consumption-orientated, then why did all of my

(Western) interviewees claim *not* to hold such a view? Why are people situating themselves in this dominant discourse of materialism and happiness? It is unlikely that 19 individuals who happened to be more 'therapeutic' than 'materialistic' were recruited for the study by coincidence; so why do people produce their accounts and make sense of their selves in such a way?

It is through the idea of *difference* that people make sense of, or produce their selves here; they are associating themselves with a non-'materialistic' identity, which is an identity or position that many other members of society are *not* seen to occupy. Lizzie, for instance, expresses this difference by saying that she is 'an exception to the rule' and thus sees herself as different from her counterparts in that she does not need to consume to be happy. 'Materialism', then, is not something *real* or absolute, but rather it is a social construct that people are using to produce their own selves through this discourse of 'difference'. The constitution of the self in these accounts thus hinges upon the comparison of oneself to a 'materialistic other'. It is this constitution of the self that is central to the dominant therapeutic discourse of happiness.

Additionally, one could also adopt concepts from Bourdieu's work on the 'symbolic economy' (Bourdieu, 1986) and argue that a non-'materialistic' view or outlook accrues or is attributed with symbolic capital, or *value* (and thus, a 'materialistic' view would be seen to *lack* value). Thus, people like Chloe and Lizzie (as well as most other interviewees), in situating themselves in this non-'materialistic' position, display particular characteristics and dispositions that correspond with this, which they are shown to do here through talk and narrative. Other respondents *performed* this by physically demonstrating in the face-to-face interview context the ways in which happiness was better achieved without material goods: Martin (32, male) stated that 'I don't wear a Rolex', before displaying his less expensive watch, Gillian (45, female) told me that she has 'never been a person who likes to wear jewellery', and Mark (41, male) talked proudly about his television that was in the room in which his interview took place: 'for the benefit of the tape, my TV has a postage-stamp size screen, it's tiny!' So it is also through displaying and embodying these characteristics in this way that people use the idea of 'materialism' to produce selves of higher value.

People are also producing *middle-class* selves through these accounts. Describing oneself as uninterested in large amounts of money, and comparing oneself to those who are, is intimately linked with the expression of a middle-class aesthetic that Bourdieu (1986) highlights in his critique of Kant's *Critique of Judgement*. Middle-class people who share this aesthetic see themselves as having 'good taste' and as having the capacity to appreciate the 'truly beautiful'; they express this in comparison to those who only have an appreciation of simple pleasures (or, a 'facile aesthetic'), which *anyone* is considered to be able to appreciate. These people are not seen to be tasteful and those who can only appreciate these pleasures are seen by the middle class to be excessive and taste*less*. Thus, by demonstrating that they do not like to spend more money on certain goods than is necessary, these respondents are expressing a middle-class aesthetic and are, in turn, producing middle-class selves.

The idea of value is also intertwined with the idea of *morality*; many respondents, in producing themselves through discourse in relation to the 'materialistic other', make sense of the non-'materialistic' stance as superior to this, or as the 'right' or more moral stance to take to happiness. Indeed, Linda's response to being asked what would make her happier was illustrative of this:

> LH: *If you could be given anything to make you feel happy or happier right now, what would it be?*
> Linda (65, female): Money, I think. It sounds very mercenary, doesn't it! But I've just been watching the news, and the state of the country... I mean, although I'm quite happy, I don't feel I've got... oh, this sounds pathetic actually, I feel guilty saying this... but I don't think I've got an enormous amount of financial security. And I think more would help me... I really feel guilty saying that, because I've got a roof over my head that belongs to me, so I'm not... but I just think more money, really. And I think I'd really be happy if I had lots more money, because then I could help my children out, you know, 'cos they're struggling a bit. You know... because my daughter-in-law's just been made redundant, and if I had more money, I could sort of help them a little bit. And my daughter's not very well off either... I just think I could help them, yeah, yeah.

Linda expressed a feeling of *guilt* about saying that she needed more money and described her admission as 'pathetic'. She may have felt like this because identification with a more 'materialistic' identity in this way meant, for her, that she was identifying with a disposition considered to be of little use-value and, furthermore, of no *moral* value (as it is associated with greed), which she would have felt reluctant to display. Additionally, she then went on to explain that money would make her happier because it would enable her to offer her children financial assistance; this may have been a further attempt to display particular characteristics both to myself as the interviewer as well as to herself that pertain to the idea that she is not a *truly* 'materialistic' person, as she draws happiness from spending money on others, which she may have considered as more moral than spending on herself. Again then, this account demonstrates the way in which Linda produced her self through discourse and talk about orientation to happiness and money which she did via the display of non-'materialistic' characteristics and dispositions.

Other respondents also provided accounts that suggested that the idea of materialism is underpinned by morality. Both Laurence and Eileen, for instance, talked about the past:

LH: Do you think that people today are happier than in the past?

Laurence (65, male): They should be, but they don't seem to be. But I think mainly, it's because they're so...well, we've got very materialistic. They seem to think that will make us happy. You know, must have a third television, must have a second car, must have this, must have that. And if you think about it, you don't really need those things. It's nice to have them. But not need them. And I think we've got very...selfish in our attitudes. You know, you might see somebody in the road, might say hello to them if they're not looking very happy. But people just don't do that anymore. Whereas many years ago, we did...Class has also changed, you know, people used to be put into groups of classes which is not there anymore. Not so much, anyway. You know, he knows his place, I know my place. So in a way that person was content with what they'd got, but we're not anymore 'cos we've seen what the other side is, so we want it. We don't need it but we've got to have it.

LH: Do you think that the idea of happiness has changed over time or over history?

Eileen (63, female): Oh yes, people are far more materialistic today than they ever were. I mean, I grew up...I won't say I was underprivileged or anything, but...everything now, with children, is I want, I want. So they grow up like that...unless they get it, they're not happy. And I think it starts from an early age, actually. You know, when I was young, we didn't get all those things. You didn't have a plastic card, you couldn't say I want it, so I'll have it. You just didn't do that. If you had the money, you could have it, buy it outright. Then you can forget about it, you've paid for it. But today, it's not like that at all, is it?

LH: *Would you say that people were happy without all those things?*

Eileen (63, female): Oh definitely, yes. There was also a camaraderie, with people...you helped one another then. People are not so ready now, to help one another. You know, there's a lot of jealousy, which is the worst thing. People are quick to run somebody else down, they'd rather be talking about somebody else and running them down. When I was young, you had good mates, you had your best friends and you were happy together. But, there's all this...it's just materialistic, with a lot of people.

Again then, Laurence situated himself within this non-'materialistic' discourse; in giving his account, he displayed appropriate characteristics and dispositions and does so by referring to a 'they' (that is, the rest of society) as the 'materialistic other' before expressing his own, different view that material things are not necessary for happiness. His account also suggests that materialism is accorded with little moral value, as he feels that society's increased consumerism is accompanied with an increased level of selfishness. Both of these, for him, have led to communitarian decline in recent years; by comparing this to – perhaps 'better' – times in the past when interaction within communities did exist, and by highlighting the way in which people might desire material goods that are unavailable to them, he has made sense of his self by displaying that he is not part of the 'materialistic other', but instead, associates with a non-'materialistic' identity that is of higher moral value.

Eileen, like Laurence, also situated herself within a non-'materialistic' discourse. Again, she identified a 'materialistic other' and expressed her difference from them by reflecting on the way in which she experienced happiness when she was younger *without* having a lot of money. Her account also implies that materialism is of little moral value, as she associated it with an increasing amount of jealousy, selfishness and conflict between individuals, as opposed to people being happy within cohesive friendship groups. Like Laurence then, she differentiated herself from the 'other', positioning herself as separate from the communal decay that she describes and therefore displaying a more moral identity.

So why does the use of this non-'materialistic' discourse of happiness accrue so much value and morality in this way? And conversely, why is the idea that material goods bring about happiness seen to *lack* value and morality? This may appear counterintuitive; within the framework of Bourdieu's symbolic economy, the acquisition of money and material goods would provide economic capital and high exchange-value (Bourdieu, 1986). Instead, however, his typology has been upturned or reversed; the accounts of these people demonstrate that material possessions, or economic capital, accrues little exchange-value, and it is *non*-'materialistic' selves that are accorded value – in the form of *cultural* capital (which is converted into symbolic capital), or use-value. In other words, people, in situating themselves in a non-'materialistic' discourse by displaying their difference from an inferior 'materialistic other', generate a sense of self-worth. As highlighted earlier in the chapter, this non-'materialistic' way of thinking is intimately related to – and can even be considered an aspect of – therapeutic discourse, through its emphasis on refraining from relying on 'external' factors for the experience of happiness. Against a backdrop of therapeutic culture, to 'know oneself' as a particularly non-'materialistic' self who looks inward – rather than outward – for their happiness would have great currency (Hazleden, 2003, Rimke, 2000) and would be accorded value. Thus, it could be said that the accrual of use-value, self-worth and cultural capital for the non-'materialistic' self is very much channelled and directed by therapeutic culture. Therefore, it is therapeutic culture itself that provides access to this cultural discourse (of non-'materialism') and practices with which experiences and perceptions of happiness are constructed and with which selves are produced. Middle-class people who situate themselves in this non-'materialistic' discourse could also be said to be expressing a middle-class aesthetic

(Bourdieu, 1986); I will show later in this chapter how and why identifying as not 'materialistic' is a distinctly middle-class way of thinking.

Money, freedom, self

Whilst it is clear that 'materialism' is considered by many to be a barrier to happiness, and that it is *non*-'materialistic' selves that are accorded value in terms of being happy, many people felt that money *is* important for the experience of happiness in certain aspects of life. Several people spoke about the way in which, despite feeling that money is not important for happiness, having *some* (that is, enough for basics like food and shelter) is indeed necessary. Alan and Danielle both expressed this:

> *LH*: *Do you think that we need money and a lot of possessions in order to be happy?*
>
> Alan (48, male): No. No, I wouldn't say you need a lot of it, I'd say not having it can be tough, having enough to ... live on, I mean, why do you need ... most people don't have a drug habit that I'm aware of ... once you've got a certain amount of money, you can afford to do ... you know, some relatively normal things, or what I consider normal, anyway ... going on holiday as a family, or having enough money to occasionally socialise with friends ... so things that I find make me happy, I'd say if that's sufficient, then you have enough. I don't need two houses. If I had lots of money, would I buy another house? Well, probably, because I've got to do something with it! Do you know what I mean? It's not necessarily per se going to make me happy.
>
> *LH*: *Do you think that we need money and a lot of possessions to be happy?*
>
> Danielle (26, female): I think everyone would want to be seen to be saying that you don't need money to be happy. But I think ... you do to an extent, so that you're comfortable enough to be able to live the life that you want to lead. So if you want to go to the cinema and then for a meal out afterwards, that you can, and not worry about the cost of that. But I've not been brought up with a lot of material ... possessions, or brand-new cars or anything. So to me, I don't have great expectations of how much money I want to earn so that I can have a 2.5 million pound

house and three cars and a swimming pool, because that's just not important to me.

Alan highlights the way in which having some money is important for being happy; he identifies a number of activities that this would enable him to do, which he considers to be 'normal' (which also suggests a normative undercurrent to happiness, where it is considered 'normal' to seek happiness via social means – see Chapter 5 for further discussion of this). However, by then going on to say that he does not need two houses, he situates himself within the non-'materialistic' discourse by displaying such preferences and thus producing a self of greater value. Danielle's account is similar to Alan's; she also identifies a number of instances in which money could provide happiness. However, she begins her account by explicitly identifying the way in which a non-'materialistic' stance might be accorded more moral value by many people. She then goes on to produce her own self in this exact way, by displaying her own non-'materialistic' characteristics and positioning herself in this discourse. Thus, contradictions arose in the way in which non-'materialistic' selves were produced, inasmuch as money may play a more prominent role than perhaps some have suggested.

Further, some respondents highlighted the way in which having a requisite amount of money brings about happiness inasmuch as it provides the individual with a sense of *freedom*:

LH: Do you feel happy at the moment?

Beth (23, female): Like, right now? I'm quite happy . . . but I think I'd be happier if I was just more settled, and had work, and things like that. Only day-to-day. But yeah, I'm happy, got good friends and family, so . . . yeah. Well I'm not unhappy! I could be happier . . . but I'm not unhappy.

LH: OK. What is it about getting a job that you think would make you happier?

Beth (23, female): It's just freedom, basically, I don't have any freedom. I'm living in somebody else's space, and that's fine with them, but it's for me really, I have a problem with it, more than I think they do. Yeah, just freedom . . . with money too, and my own space, I'd be freer. I wouldn't be so self-conscious all the time. If I had more money, I could do all of the things I wanted to do...Yeah, just being able to get up and go a bit more than I can now.

LH: *If you could be given anything to make you feel happy or happier right now, what would it be?*

Tom (25, male): Erm...a good, full-time, reasonably well-paid job! A full-time job would be good as I'm only part-time at the moment. Yeah, a full-time job preferably in the charity sector, fundraising. That's what I want most at the moment. You know, if you said that I'll meet a long-term girlfriend next week, then that would be nice, but I'd really like a job! I need a job to get the money to be able to do things that I want to do. Like, I live at home, but I want to move out and be independent...I'd like to go travelling for a bit maybe, but I need that full-time job to do that. That's what I really want right now.

Beth, who was unemployed and was lodging temporarily on a friend's couch at the time of the interview, talks about feeling unhappy about the lack of freedom that accompanies her lack of work and money. Despite situating herself in a non-'materialistic' discourse at other points during her interview, she did not do so here. She had clearly reflected on this previously and describes feeling self-conscious (this type of self-reflection being a major aspect of therapeutic culture – see Chapter 4 for further discussion of this). Tom, like Beth, also describes his dissatisfaction with his employment circumstances and expresses a desire for more independence and freedom than his current salary allows for; he is thus also not situating himself within non-'materialistic' discourse here.

These accounts thus appear contradictory to those presented hitherto in this chapter. Freedom – as discussed in detail in Chapter 5 – has been shown to be intimately related to the idea of happiness, and the two are very much associated in people's accounts of their experiences and perceptions of happiness. Indeed, freedom is often considered to be a condition of happiness (see Chapter 5 for further discussion); it is also a fundamental aspect of therapeutic culture. Thus, essentially, these accounts are suggesting that *some* money is necessary for being happy. Why is money considered to be important for freedom (and thus happiness), when non-'materialistic' discourse also plays such a prominent role in accounts of happiness? Freedom and non-materialism are clearly both important aspects of therapeutic culture, but surely these are contradictory if money is seen to be necessary for freedom?

Whilst money is considered important for freedom and happiness, these accounts are not suggesting that *a lot* of money is necessary. An overwhelmingly dominant discourse amongst all respondents was that of 'enough' money being a necessity for happiness, but that of 'too much' being problematic. That is to say that after accounting for the necessity of a small amount of money, non-'materialistic' selves are still accorded moral value in people's accounts of happiness. People nevertheless produce their selves in relation to this 'materialistic other' that is characterised by the want of material goods *beyond* that which is considered 'normal', and beyond that of freedom, basic subsistence and comfort. Thus, people continue to replay normative, non-'materialistic' discourses whilst simultaneously expressing a desire to accrue more wealth.

(Non-)'Materialistic' self-production: Therapeutic culture and social class

Many people, then, in reflecting upon the relationship between money and happiness, expressed the idea that money and consumption are not important for a happy life; in other words, they produce non-'materialistic' selves. The concept of such a self rests on the widespread belief that one ought not to depend upon 'external' sources for their happiness, but instead, should draw it from 'within', via technologies of, or 'work' upon, the self; the production of this kind of self is thus a form of self-knowledge. It is in this way then, that this self-production is intimately interwoven with, and an aspect of, therapeutic culture. Non-'materialistic' selves are thus accorded more moral value than 'materialistic' selves, who would – against the fundamental precepts of therapeutic culture – draw happiness from 'outside' the self; indeed, it is via the process of 'work' on the self that non-'materialistic' selves accrue value. Therefore it is evident here that people's perceptions of happiness and money are formed against a backdrop of therapeutic culture. However, *class* also has a direct impact here: whilst therapeutic culture is an important aspect of this self-production, it is also an expression of a middle-class aesthetic, whereby selves are produced via discourses of difference from other, more 'tasteless', 'excessive' selves (Lawler, 2005) who require money and possessions to be happy. It could be argued here, then, that this is a dominant way in which middle-class people make sense of their happiness in relation to money. They may regard others, particularly those from lower classes, as 'tasteless' and 'excessive' in this way. Furthermore, emphasising the importance of drawing happiness from 'inside' the self, rather than from an external factor such as money, could also be said to be a distinctly middle-class conception of happiness. Therefore, therapeutic discourse may said to be a middle-class way of making sense of the world.

So in this analysis, materialism is not a 'real' concept as such; that is, there is no absolute 'materialism metric' against which it can be measured. Rather, it is a construct upon which people (and specifically middle-class people) draw when making sense of their experiences and perceptions of happiness and money, as well as producing their selves in this particular way. They do this first, in displaying non-'materialistic' characteristics and dispositions, second, when positioning themselves in discourses around difference from a 'materialistic other' and third, when drawing upon discourses around the importance of having 'enough' money for the attainment of comfort and freedom. It would be highly useful to have an understanding of the ways in which people from other class backgrounds make sense of money and their happiness; however, this is unfortunately outside the scope of this book and is a subject for a further study.

So, the analysis presented in this chapter shows that the relationship between money and happiness is far from straightforward. The production of the self, when considered in relation to such a framework, is complex; people express a need or want for a requisite amount of money, but do so whilst continuing to position themselves within this normative non-'materialistic' discourse. The 'work' on the self that is performed in doing so enables such selves to accrue value. Therapeutic culture – as well as the middle-class aesthetic – frame both this accrual of value to, and the production of, non-materialist selves; it is both of these that provide access to the discourses and dispositions with which experiences and perceptions of the happiness of middle-class people are constructed.

Fulfilling employment

Working life has also been identified by many people as being of high importance for being happy. In particular, it is feelings of *fulfilment* and *achievement* that contribute to their happiness, rather than any monetary or financial gains that their work may bring. In a Marxist sense, it is a relationship with one's 'species being' and sense of identity that is important for happiness, as well as a sense of one's work being more than simply a means of survival (Marx and Engels, 1988). This resonates with people's orientations to money that were highlighted in the preceding section: rather than money *per se* being a source of happiness, it is the intrinsic enjoyment of work that is important, as well as the way in which the work process may modify and strengthen one's sense of self. Again, it will be shown here how this is a distinctly middle-class way of reconciling happiness and work.

There is thus a therapeutic cultural ideal towards which people seem to be aspiring, whereby the relationship between one's experience of happiness and their working lives is underpinned by feelings of achievement and self-fulfilment; in other words, it is not money that is considered to bring about happiness, but an internal sense of heightened *self-knowledge*. Although not everyone actually achieves this feeling of fulfilment, but instead feels a sense of *alienation* from their work (as will be demonstrated later in this section), many nevertheless express a desire for or an aspiration towards it.

As well as being a therapeutic cultural ideal, it is also a *middle-class* ideal whereby – for the middle classes at least – a shift has occurred from the commodity fetishism, or the objectification of money, acknowledged by Karl Marx (1867/1999), to a concern with a more intrinsic, self-orientated evaluation of the work process. Again, as explored in the previous section, this intrinsic evaluation of work is bound up with the middle-class aesthetic and the production of middle class, 'tasteful' selves; people do not express any desire for money and consumption because this is intimately linked with working-class *excess* and *lack* of taste, which, according to Bourdieu (1986), in his critical analysis of Kant's 'Critique of Judgement', is lacking in moral worth.

Indeed, Mark talked about the happiness and fulfilment that he has experienced through his work, despite the fact that he is 'paid peanuts':

Mark (41, male): I have a nice flat, and a great job that I love,
I work for a charity, I get paid peanuts, but I'm lucky in the

respect, as I said, with my job that I wake up on a Monday morning and think 'yeah, it's Monday!', in fact, at the times when I'm unhappy, certainly over the last few months, and looking back, they've been periods of time when I haven't been working. Or even a weekend off, it's like sometimes I won't leave the settee on a weekend off and feel really miserable, but then going to work on Monday makes me feel happy, 'cos I'm doing things and getting a buzz out of my work and stuff.

Mark expresses his feelings towards his work by positioning himself in another discourse of *difference*; he describes himself as 'lucky' to have a fulfilling job, which suggests that he considers himself to be unusual in this respect. He thus positions himself as something different to the norm. Again, this is a *classed* position; by emphasising that he is satisfied despite the fact that he is paid 'peanuts', he produces his *middle-class self* by distancing himself from any reliance upon wealth for his happiness. As discussed in the preceding section, a need and a want for money and consumption is associated – in relation to Bourdieu's critique of Kantian aesthetics – with a 'tasteless', working class, facile aesthetic that is seen to lack any moral value (Bourdieu, 1986). Further, work could also, for Mark, facilitate his utilisation of a technology of the self (Foucault, 1988); going to work after a 'weekend off' is a resource that he draws upon to work on himself and maximise his happiness (which he is unable to do when at home on his settee).

Alan, when asked about the happiest person he knows, emphasised an acquaintance's fulfilment at work, which he considered to be the central factor to his happiness:

LH: Who is the happiest person you know, and why?
Alan (48, male): [pauses] I think I know a couple of blokes who are really quite happy. They're very successful in their careers, extremely successful ... so they have an awful lot of – within their industry – fame and influence ... and one of them is extremely well financially rewarded. But I don't think that's what makes him happy, I think it's this fact that they get this ... high level of achievement, satisfaction in what they do. And I think that's made them quite happy.

Like Mark, Alan also replays a normative, classed discourse; whilst he acknowledges that income *could* be a source of happiness, he infers that the source of his acquaintance's happiness is more likely to be intrinsic job satisfaction than the money that he earns. Again, he may have said this because an association between large amounts of money and happiness is considered excessive, 'tasteless' and lacking in middle-class aesthetic (Bourdieu, 1986) and thus accorded with less value.

Lizzie described her happiness with her working life:

> Lizzie (25, female): I think my career is going really well for me at the moment. About six months ago I was in a secretarial role for the Director of Communications at [government department] and when he got promoted, I had the opportunity to move, to get rid of the secretarial role, and start at the bottom of press and marketing which is an area that I really want to get into. So I'm kind of in the process at the moment of... even though I get called a press and marketing officer, I'm a little bit below that role, but I'm being trained up by people that I really respect a lot, and have good relationships with all my colleagues... they're kind of training me up at the moment and they're really helping me and mentoring me and kind of showing me the ropes for the things that I need to do to be able to get up to the next level in my career. So even though I'm not quite there yet, I'm at a stage of my life where I finally know what I want to do... for the moment, and I'm achieving it at the moment.

Again, for Lizzie, work facilitates her use of a technology of the self (Foucault, 1988); although she did not feel fulfilled in her previous role as a secretary, her promotion allowed her to strengthen her understanding of her path in life, which made her feel happy. Furthermore, this understanding is a form of self-knowledge, and it thus allowed her to strengthen her relationship with her self and her identity. It is in this way that she situates herself within therapeutic discourse. In addition to this, Lizzie's account is also – implicitly – reflective of a middle-class aesthetic; she emphasises the sense of achievement that she gets from her work, but does not – at any point – attribute any of her happiness to the money that she earns. By drawing attention specifically to the happiness that she experiences from the *intrinsic* aspects of her job, she produces a specifically middle-class self, for whom an excessive amount of wealth is of low importance.

Thus, the three extracts presented here all show the way in which people produce their selves via their relation to the middle-class aesthetic (Bourdieu, 1986, Lawler, 2005). In other words, people in each of these accounts have positioned themselves as *distinct* or *separate* from an identity for which large amounts of money and 'excess' (which may, for them, be seen to represent working-class 'tastelessness') are associated with happiness. Instead, they produce their middle-class selves by identifying with an aspiration for intrinsic fulfilment and satisfaction from work and economic life.

However, they have all done so within a therapeutic cultural framework; for some, work enables people to draw upon a technology of the self (Foucault, 1988) via which they are able to maximise their self-knowledge and strengthen their relationships with their selves. Ideally, they would be autonomous, choosing individuals who have a capacity to seek and gain fulfilment in order to heighten such self-knowledge (Beck, 1992, Giddens, 1991, Rose, 1996). One can thus see that it is therapeutic discourse that people are using when articulating their experiences of happiness and work, and that therapeutic discourse is a distinctly middle-class way of doing this. However, it may not always be as straightforward as this.

Fulfilling work may be an ideal that many people highlight in their accounts of happiness; indeed, as shown above, this illustrates the centrality of therapeutic culture to such accounts. However, it is not necessarily accessible to all; that is, not everyone is granted the capacity to be *able* to gain such intrinsic fulfilment. It is in this way that therapeutic discourse (and more specifically, therapeutic cultural resources and ideals) is only available to those in more privileged socio-economic positions. Some respondents highlight examples where they have not been able to heighten their self-knowledge in this way. Tom, for instance, expresses unhappiness at the *lack* of freedom and independence that his work brings about:

> LH: *If you could be given anything to make you feel happy or happier right now, what would it be?*
> Tom (25, male): Erm ... a good, full-time, reasonably well-paid job! A full-time job would be good as I'm only part-time at the

moment. Yeah, a full-time job preferably in the charity sector, fundraising...where I can get a sense of achievement that I'm doing an interesting job. That's what I want most at the moment. You know, if you said that I'll meet a long-term girlfriend next week, then that would be nice, but I'd really like a job! I need a job to get the money to be able to do things that I want to do. Like, I live at home, but I want to move out and be independent...I'd like to travel a bit maybe, but I need that full-time job to do that. That's what I really want right now.

Tom talks about the way in which his employment situation has denied him access to the therapeutic cultural ideals of autonomy and choice. Although he acknowledges a desire for freedom and fulfilment (which he feels that he could get if he had a full-time job), his account suggests that he is not an autonomous individual who is able to work on himself and heighten his self-knowledge. This raises the question of whether there may be shortcomings in some of the 'therapeutic turn' literature: the self, rather than being completely autonomous and free to work on him or herself in order to become a 'better' person, is actually *constrained* by its social position; that is, different selves have differential access (according to their position) to the resources and practices with which to work on their selves (Savage, 2000, Skeggs, 2004), and only those in more advantaged positions are able to do this. Indeed, Tom's situation and social position do not allow him access to such resources and practices, although he acknowledges a desire for this.

Martin also talks about his feelings towards his recent lack of success:

Martin (32, male): I wonder what would make me happier at the moment...it's difficult to say. If you'd asked me three years ago, the way things were going, I was close to becoming a banker, I was interviewing with [Bank Y]...I'm happy having the job I have at the moment, and I don't think I have the strength to be working harder, I mean I work a nine to five job, I get paid well, I don't think I'd have the energy at the moment to go back to [Bank X], it would just run me into the ground. But at the same time, the fact that I don't feel that I have the energy anymore...and maybe it's because of my age...it kind of erodes my happiness as well. 'Cos at one point I thought I was going to be a really successful... after graduating I got a job, then I got a better job, then I got another better job, and before I knew it people were offering me one hundred thousand pound base salaries with fifty per cent guaranteed bonuses. So I felt close to becoming a very successful person. Then in the last year that kind of all got knocked away, and now I'm basically back to where I was three or four years ago, when I got my first job... I'm fine with that, it's the middle of a recession... But at the time it disaffected my confidence... [...] But I'm wise enough to know that that applies for a lot of people... I know shitloads of guys who have lost their jobs. But I would have probably hoped that I would have achieved a bit more by now, or at least that I would have had less setbacks in terms of things that have happened in the last year that I feel have undermined me...

Martin, like Tom, acknowledges a desire and aspiration for fulfilment and achievement in his working life. This is especially evident in his admission that 'I would have probably hoped that I would have achieved a bit more by now', which suggests that he has previously undertaken extensive reflection on what kind of self he is and would like to be. Indeed, he talks about times in the past when he did experience this and does so in a self-orientated, therapeutic fashion; rather than describing these experiences simply as events, Martin's account suggests that work for him is something that he sees to be central to his identity and to his cultivation of a 'healthy' and positive relationship with his self (Hazleden, 2003), inasmuch as he had a high regard for himself and felt like a 'very successful person'. His perceived current decline in status impacted on his confidence. Thus, he has situated himself within therapeutic discourse in talking about his experiences of happiness in his working life.

Again, however, Martin described feeling unhappy and lacking in confidence about having experienced diminished fulfilment from his work in recent years. He identified a number of factors, in particular his age, that may have contributed to this. His account thus suggests that, like Tom, his social position is restricting his access to the resources and practices   within his working life at least – with which he can be the autonomous, fulfilled individual that he aspires to be, and which therapeutic culture advocates (Savage, 2000, Skeggs, 2004).

Sophie describes the unhappiness that she experiences in relation to her work as a receptionist for a large pensions company and explains why she would like another job:

> *LH*: *You said earlier that you'd like a career change – why is that?*
> Sophie (22, female): Because...I want to broaden my mind... I also want to feel a part of something, you know. Like, at the moment, I don't feel a buzz from work...Imagine that you work as a journalist or something, and you get a real buzz – I don't have that. I'd just like to do something varied, that's not the same every day, where I'm not bottom of the pile. And my team, the admin team...we're like the shit team, we get the shit jobs... And they're so boring, like booking meeting rooms...it's not something that anyone ever says 'well done' for, I never get any thanks, I never feel like anyone appreciates what I do, you know. And I think all the partners probably think I have nothing going for me...that I'm stupid. The girls on my team all seem to be really dissatisfied as well, and none of them have any drive or creativity. Like, we all have to wear these matching suits, you know, and I really don't feel like an individual because of that, I can't express who I am. To be honest, I'm really dreading going into work tomorrow...

Sophie, like Tom and Martin, also expressed an aspiration for fulfilment at work; she talked about wanting a career change to something more fulfilling than her current job, which does not allow her to experience or to even seek fulfilment. She expresses further frustration at the impression she has that the partners in her company *perceive* her as having no ambition for any achievement. That is to say, one source of her unhappiness at work is the identity that her superiors have assigned to her (which is an unintelligent, unambitious individual). Whilst in this account, she expresses a middle-class aesthetic, by highlighting a desire for fulfilment and by distancing herself from any claims of the monetary benefits of work, she may fear that it is the very outlook (or the tasteless, working-class, facile aesthetic (Bourdieu, 1986)) that she is positioning herself as distinct from that is that which her colleagues (mis)assign to her. Further, she even goes as far as expressing *disgust* (Lawler, 2005) towards the low-status administration team of which she is a part ('we're like the shit team, we get the shit jobs'); although she is very much a member of the team, she also disassociates herself from it by describing her team-mates as lacking in 'drive or creativity' whilst simultaneously highlighting her own drive to seek a new job in which she could use some of her own creativity. Thus, whilst the rest of her team may – for Sophie at least – seem to only express a facile aesthetic, and are dissatisfied in their jobs, Sophie herself expresses her unhappiness by distancing herself from this type of outlook, and instead, expresses a middle-class aesthetic by stating that she would like to seek further fulfilment and satisfaction in her working life, rather than choosing to stay in her job because it provides a steady income.

Despite the fact that Sophie lacks access to the resources and practices with which to gain fulfilment and self-knowledge through her work, she also positions herself within therapeutic discourse in her account. This is particularly evident inasmuch as she would *like* to be able to work on herself in order to experience job satisfaction. One aspect of her work that she is unhappy with is the suit uniform that she and other members of her team are made to wear; she is unhappy about the fact that wearing the suit prevents her from feeling like an individual and expressing herself. Not only is she alienated from her sense of identity, self or 'species-being' in this way (Marx and Engels, 1988), but she is also, again, denied access to resources and practices with which to work on herself and heighten her self-knowledge. She nevertheless acknowledges that this is an ideal that she aspires towards in her working life. For Sophie, being happy is intimately linked with feeling like 'an individual', self-expression and a strengthened relationship with her self (Hazleden, 2003).

Thus, Sophie, Martin and Tom are all in problematic positions whereby they possess a desire for fulfilling, satisfying work (rather than simply a job that pays well), but simultaneously lack access to the resources and practices with which to achieve this fulfilment (and gain any heightened self-knowledge that may accompany it).

It is evident, then, that therapeutic discourse *is* used by people in their accounts of happiness and their working lives. This is particularly the case with regard to their accounts of fulfilment; for people who *do* experience this, their work can be considered a technology of the self (Foucault, 1988), in that the work process enables them to achieve, work on themselves and heighten their self-knowledge. However, whilst a large number of people *aspire* for such fulfilment, access to it is not available to all; for some, their social position prevents them from accessing the resources and practices with which it can be sought and experienced.

People's accounts of such experiences of fulfilment have also been shown to be *classed*. This is the case in two ways; firstly, people have differential access to the resources and practices that enable them to experience fulfilment according to their class position (Savage, 2000, Skeggs, 2004) (though this is not always limited to class, as we have seen: this can also be the case with regard to gender, age, race and sexuality). Secondly, discourses of fulfilment from work more generally are inextricably bound up with the middle-class aesthetic; by positioning oneself in such a discourse, one is also positioning themselves as *separate* or *distinct* from an identity which associates money and wealth with happiness, and which may be perceived as excessive, 'tasteless' and associated with the working class's facile aesthetic (Bourdieu, 1986). It is in giving these kinds of accounts, then, that people produce their (middle) classed selves.

People's accounts of money, working life and happiness, then, are bound up with both therapeutic culture and the middle-class aesthetic; however, the relationship between therapeutic culture and social class is a complex one. On the one hand, perceiving experiences of happiness as internal and restricted to that of the individual, and seeking to know more about oneself in order to improve one's relationship with their self, may all be subjective processes that are found amongst people in a variety of social positions, whether or not they have access to the resources with which they can do so. On the other, however, particular accounts and discourses pertaining to money, wealth, fulfilment and happiness may be utilised more by the middle classes. The idea that happiness should come from 'within', rather from external factors such as money, which is a precept very much rooted within therapeutic discourse, is a distinctly middle-class one. This analysis shows that middle-class people in particular, like those who were interviewed, use therapeutic discourse to articulate their experiences and perceptions of happiness, money and work.

Conclusion

People's working lives and financial situations are clearly central to their experiences and perceptions of happiness. As has been demonstrated in this chapter, discourses are used by people in producing their accounts of these; this is done with particular use of therapeutic discourse and a middle-class aesthetic.

People thus use therapeutic discourse in constructing their accounts of happiness, money and working life. In terms of orientations to money, people's assertions that money should not be a source of happiness rest upon the wider therapeutic precept whereby happiness ought to be experienced as something individual, internal and natural. Thus, according to this precept, happiness should not be sought from any sources external to the individual (such as money). Similarly, people's accounts of happiness and their working lives largely centre around the ideas of fulfilment and achievement, rather than the money they earn per se. The accounts of the fulfilment and achievement that are experienced by interviewees (or in some cases, that are not experienced but aspired for) suggest that for many, work facilitates the utilisation of a technology of the self (Foucault, 1988) whereby people use their experiences at work to 'work' on themselves and seek happiness and self-actualisation. Whilst this fulfilment is not achieved by all, it is something that many expressed a desire for (and indeed, lack of fulfilment was often expressed as *un*happiness). So, whilst much of the 'therapeutic turn' literature assumes that everyone is able to be an autonomous, choosing individual who can draw upon technologies with which to heighten their self-knowledge, access to the resources and practices with which this can be achieved is not necessarily available to all, and many people are unable to draw happiness from their working lives. Nevertheless, a desire and aspiration for a gain of self-knowledge via one's working life is something that was expressed by the majority of respondents.

However, *class* has also played a role in the production of people's accounts of happiness here. In particular, people often expressed the middle-class aesthetic which Bourdieu (1986) highlights in his critique of Kant's *Critique of Judgement*. With regard to their perceptions of money and happiness, the expression of the widespread view that very large amounts of money and wealth may be a hindrance to happiness is one way in which people positioned themselves as *distinct* or different from an 'other' who may choose to spend money on expensive consumer goods and who may be considered 'tasteless' and 'excessive'. Similarly, they placed emphasis on feelings of fulfilment and achievement in their accounts of happiness and their working lives in order to distance themselves from the 'tasteless, excessive other' which may prioritise money and salary over more intrinsic satisfaction. So by positioning themselves within discourses of fulfilment in this way, they produce such middle class, 'tasteful' identities. It is in this way that people produce their – middle-class – selves in these accounts of happiness, via the expression of a classed aesthetic, within a framework of therapeutic culture. Thus, it can be shown that the relationship between money, work and happiness is a complex one, but that the use of discourse in the production of accounts surrounding this is fundamental to an understanding of happiness.

7
Conclusion

The way in which people produce their accounts of their experiences and perceptions of happiness is surrounded by a number of complexities, as this book has shown. They do so via the use of a number of dominant discourses or narratives, and it is by doing so that a shared cultural sense of what happiness 'is' is created. That is to say, people's accounts of happiness are not simply indicative or reflective of private, individual thoughts, but rather, they are constructed and articulated via culturally specific ways of being and thinking.

The book has also demonstrated that many of the determinants of happiness that have been highlighted in the 'science of happiness' literature (see Chapter 2) are both highly relevant and central to people's experiences of it; indeed, all interviewees acknowledged factors such as family, friends, working life and money in their accounts, often without being prompted or asked. However, what has also been indicated is that these determinants are not necessarily discrete categories that can bring about feelings or experiences of happiness in a singular way. Rather, they should be considered as interlinked and interrelated whereby together they make up a complex framework within which the experience and perception of happiness is located. A further layer of complexity is added when happiness is explored through the lens of dominant cultural discourse that this book adopts; in producing accounts of happiness through discourse in this way, linkages and tensions between different determinants emerge, rendering the experience of happiness a multifaceted one. It is, therefore, not as linear and straightforward as some of the happiness literature suggests.

This final chapter of the book revisits some of its central ideas, offering a reflection on what we have learned about what happiness is and what it means to people. It also considers the ways in which this knowledge contributes to that already known in sociology and happiness studies, and how such an understanding of happiness can be of use in government policymaking.

The social construction of happiness

What do people understand happiness to be? All of those interviewed were asked about what they felt that happiness is, and all positioned themselves within dominant discourses when producing accounts in response to this question. Indeed, a range of discourses was often drawn upon simultaneously. Some of the discourses that were drawn upon constituted happiness as *asocial*, that is, immune and resistant to social factors. One of these was a discourse of elusiveness, whereby happiness, like with love, was described as being 'knowable only intuitively, at the level of feeling' (Jackson, 1999:100). It was also made sense of as something for which there is no straightforward, clear-cut way in which it can be defined. Many people situated themselves within discourses of naturalness and biology; that is, happiness was seen to come from within the body. It was in this way that the body was seen to be a kind of 'container' for happiness (Lupton, 1998). Happiness was therefore reified through this discourse, as something that is tangible, real and existing within the body. This discourse also gives rise to the idea that that it is one's own personal *responsibility* to change their life and to find a solution to problems, and that *dependency* on sources external to oneself is undesirable. This was expressed particularly with regard to psychiatric medication such as anti-depressants; an overall tenet of this discourse was that people who are not happy should be capable of regaining their happiness 'naturally' rather than 'artificially', via medication. The idea that happiness is 'natural' was also expressed in relation to its presence across time and space. Whilst a number of social changes and processes that have taken place in contemporary Western society were identified, such as increased consumerism and a growing emphasis on the importance of body image, that have affected what might *make* us happy, some respondents felt that the actual *experience* of happiness would withstand such changes, as it is 'natural' and 'internal'.

A discourse of uniqueness was also widely used by respondents, whereby happiness is conceived as something that each individual would experience differently, despite the fact that a large number of them expressed this same idea. It was described as being manifested through one's personality and is understood to play a key role in the way in which one constructs and reconstructs their personal identity.

As well as being constituted as asocial, other discourses were used in producing accounts of what happiness is, which were characterised by the locating of happiness within a complex normative framework in which there exists cultural guidelines on the way in which happiness ought to be displayed and experienced. Many people situated themselves within the discourse of positive thinking, a discourse whose roots are in self-help literature. The fundamental tenet of it is that happiness is something that should be universally striven for in life, and that people should attempt to be happy even in adverse circumstances. Simultaneously, however, many interviewees positioned themselves within the discourse of transience, which is based upon the idea that negative or unpleasant experiences are an inevitable part of life, and therefore one cannot and should not expect to be happy at all times. Furthermore, periodic feelings of unhappiness or misery are often beneficial, in order that experiences of happiness can be fully appreciated, and an excess of happiness may be regarded as 'unnatural' or inauthentic. Therefore, whilst it might be deemed as undesirable to be persistently depressed (as this would run counter to the positive thinking discourse), positioning oneself within this discourse of transience would also suggest an undesirability of persistent *happiness*. It is in this way that these two discourses render the display and experience of happiness subject to negotiation and 'balance' of these – often implicit – guidelines.

So, happiness is considered to be asocial, or immune to social, 'external' factors, and it is also understood to be located within a normative framework in which an excess or deficiency of it is undesirable. However, in relation to people's accounts of their *experiences* of happiness, the therapeutic discourse was dominant. In positioning themselves within this discourse, people understood their experiences of happiness as being individualised, internal and self-orientated. Many of the precepts of this discourse have their roots in the self-help and therapy industries. In particular, the self is considered as having a specific relation to itself; that is, it is considered to be 'ontologically separate' from the individual (Hazleden, 2003:416). It is also the primary site on which individuals are able to 'work', and on which they can perform techniques or technologies in order to change or improve their sense of selfhood in some way or to increase their self-knowledge (Foucault, 1988). Central to the therapeutic discourse of happiness is the idea that self-care and self-knowledge are fundamental to being happy. Happiness is seen to be most easily achieved though the cultivation of a 'healthy relationship with the self' (Hazleden, 2003:421). Although therapeutic discourse is a quintessentially modern way of making sense of the self and of happiness (Illouz, 2007), it is, like some of the discourses used in order to produce accounts of what happiness 'is', inherently asocial. In part, this is because it is often drawn upon in tandem with the discourses of naturalness and biology; that is, happiness is seen to be 'contained' within the self or the body (see Lupton, 1998), and is considered to be a 'resource' upon which the individual can 'work', by utilising technologies or techniques of the self (see Foucault, 1988), whenever necessary. Furthermore, the individual is seen to be self-sufficient in this way; with self-sufficiency being a key aspect of self-help literature, one is regarded as being able to 'work' on their happiness without any assistance from other people or from any external bodies.

Despite the dominance and overwhelming use of such asocial discourses in producing accounts of experiences of happiness, interpersonal relationships were nevertheless considered to be important factors for a happy life. Indeed, family relationships and community and friends have been put forward by economists (such as Richard Layard (2011)) as two of the key determinants of happiness. However, these economists have not acknowledged everyday experiences of happiness. Chapter 5 demonstrated the way in which the discourses discussed here were used by people in order to produce accounts of the specific ways in which happiness is experienced in relation to interpersonal relationships. A tension became apparent with regard to people's accounts of their happiness and interpersonal relationships, whereby they were produced whilst positioned within therapeutic discourse; that is to say, that although other people were important in the participants' experiences of happiness, they articulated this via an inherently self-orientated narrative. People's accounts of the happiness that they experienced in relation to being in love and to sexual relationships were also largely asocial (with the exception of one respondent, whose conception of having a partner is intimately bound up with sociality and modern social fragmentation). Although these experiences, crucially, concerned another person, or other people, some respondents described being in love as 'more than just happiness', that is, as being a kind of 'disreality' (Barthes, 1978), disconnected from the wider social world. Sexual relationships, too, were described using a discourse of naturalness, as they were considered to be related to the satisfaction of a 'natural' and 'innate' drive. Conversely, however, the discourse surrounding the desirability of sex within an established, loving relationship over 'casual' sex that takes place outside of such a relationship was more social; people who position themselves within this may do so in order to conform to a normative expectation to be 'respectable' and to an image of legitimate heterosexuality (Skeggs, 1997). Nevertheless, such a tension between social and asocial discourses appears to exist in relation to experiences of happiness and interpersonal relationships. This may be because the central self-orientated precepts of therapeutic culture serve to obscure the aspects of human existence that are interdependent, intersubjective and social (Rimke, 2000). What is important to note here, is that the intermeshing of different discourses in this way means that the role that interpersonal relationships may play in the experience of happiness cannot be as linear or as straightforward as economists postulate. Though other people may indeed be considered to be a key ingredient for a happy life, experiences of them are still likely to be dominantly interpreted and articulated via a – partly asocial – framework of biology, naturalness and self-sufficiency.

Financial situation and working life, another of the two major determinants of happiness outlined by economists, were also described by respondents as very important for a happy life. However, as with interpersonal relationships, people situated themselves within specific dominant discourses in relation to these, and they therefore produced specific accounts of their happiness in relation to them. Again, they were shown to draw heavily on therapeutic discourse in their accounts of their working lives, particularly with regard to the pursuit of self-fulfilment. However, it was also demonstrated that therapeutic ideals such as individualisation may compete with other ideas, namely social class. Many respondents were shown, when giving accounts of their perceptions of money and happiness, to express a view that very large amounts of money and wealth may be a hindrance to happiness. They positioned themselves as *distinct* or different from an 'other' who may choose to spend money on expensive consumer goods, and who may be considered 'tasteless' and 'excessive'. Similarly, they placed emphasis on feelings of fulfilment and achievement in their accounts of happiness and their working lives in order to distance themselves from the 'tasteless, excessive other' which may prioritise money and salary over more intrinsic satisfaction. So by positioning themselves within discourses of fulfilment in this way, they produce such middle class, 'tasteful' identities via the expression of a classed aesthetic, but nevertheless through a framework of therapeutic discourse. Thus, therapeutic discourse can be seen to compete with social class in this way, but it could also be argued here that therapeutic discourse is a distinctly middle class way of understanding the world. Here, again then, financial situation and working life are made sense of and articulated via an individualised, self-orientated narrative, and the role that they may play in the experience of happiness cannot be as linear or as straightforward as economists postulate.

A bigger picture

The 'determinants' of happiness put forward by economists may not 'affect' or 'cause' happiness in the way that they suggest. Statistical analyses may yield a correlation between happiness and each of these, but they cannot necessarily be considered as singular, straightforward 'causes'. This is because happiness is underpinned by a set of complex sociocultural norms, narratives and understandings, of which these factors are a part.

This is not to say that such determinants should be rejected outright. All of the factors that are presented as determinants arose in people's qualitative accounts of happiness; indeed, many of them formed the very narratives that are so dominant in relation to happiness. That is, when asked what makes them happy, the majority of interviewees gave responses such as 'family', 'friends' and 'fulfilling work', each time naming factors that are commonly understood in Britain and in the West as being associated with happiness. Therefore, the understanding of happiness that this book has offered very much resonates with aspects of the 'science of happiness' literature, and, by shedding light on the way in which each of these factors feature in people's day-to-day experiences of happiness, it can complement, rather than stand in opposition to them. It is in this way that such a sociological understanding of happiness is so useful; it allows us to more fully appreciate the ways in which different aspects of our social worlds feature in our experiences and perceptions.

What is needed, then, is for there to be more integration of – and interaction between – different 'branches' of happiness studies. If disciplinary boundaries (between economics, psychology, sociology and so on) can be traversed, knowledge can be drawn together to yield a richer and more complete picture of the place that happiness occupies both in British society, and beyond.

Happiness policies: What can be done?

Steps are being taken by the current national government, as discussed at the start of the book, to ensure that social policy decisions can begin to be informed by happiness research. Social survey data have begun to be collected as part of the 'Measuring National Wellbeing' programme, initiated by the Office for National Statistics (ONS). However, these data are unlikely to provide the government with a complete picture of the happiness of the United Kingdom. This is because, although such data may offer an insight into general *levels* of happiness across the country, they will be unable to capture the happiness of individuals at the level of the everyday. Public policies that are formulated on the basis of such data may, as a result, be insufficiently equipped to target specific areas of people's lives that may be most in need of attention.

Nevertheless, as stated in the discussion in the previous section, combining such national data with a more sociological understanding of day-to-day happiness experiences may remedy this situation; knowledge of how happiness is made sense of by people could be of high importance for government policy. However, this is not necessarily a straightforward issue. On one hand, this book has demonstrated that interpersonal relationships and fulfilling working lives are key features in people's perceptions and experiences of happiness, and therefore a sensible step for government policymakers could be the implementation of programmes that could help to strengthen local communities, reduce levels of loneliness for some people and promote well-being at work policies. However, what is problematic is that the dominant narrative surrounding the importance of relationships for a happy life competes in many people's accounts with the idea that happiness is individual and, therefore, must come from within oneself. Thus, if it is understood to be an individual's responsibility to be happy, government policies and initiatives could potentially be ineffective. This argument could be countered by the suggestion that Richard Layard's (2011) proposal to increase the number of psychotherapists in Britain may appeal to those who make sense of their happiness through therapeutic discourse (and in some cases, this may be effective). However, taking into account the idea that scepticism has been expressed towards the therapy industry because it involves relying on something outside of one's self (and would therefore lead to 'inauthentic' happiness) raises the possibility that this could also not be completely fruitful. Therefore, it must be borne in mind that happiness is a complex experience that cannot necessarily be partnered with straightforward and universal policy solutions.

Competing debates

This book serves as a contribution to, but also as a critique of, debates on therapeutic culture. Whilst it has demonstrated the overwhelming pervasiveness of therapeutic discourse in people's accounts of happiness, thus lending support to the assertion that modern societies have witnessed a therapeutic 'turn', it must also be borne in mind that this is not necessarily a streamlined process. Other discourses may compete with this one in people's understandings of their selves and of the world around them, such as those of interpersonal relationships and of social class. Furthermore, some people may lack access to the resources and practices that allow them to be fully self-sufficient and to 'work' on their selves in order to enhance their own self-knowledge, and thus some therapeutic cultural resources may be unavailable to them. The book could also contribute to debates within the sociology of emotions, by attempting to raise the profile of happiness research within this body of literature. Currently, it is rarely acknowledged as an area of study in its own right by scholars in this subfield; instead, it often features as a more peripheral aspect of studies of emotions more generally.

A happier sociology?

So the groundwork has now been laid for the further development of a sociology of happiness. Despite happiness' lack of popularity amongst sociologists (see Chapter 1 for a detailed discussion of the reasons for this), I argue that the study of happiness should occupy a much more central position within sociology. I am not, as the subtitle of this section might imply, suggesting that sociologists become less critical or more naïve in their research; the negative outlook that they often possess is of extreme importance for allowing injustices to be brought to the fore, as well as for problematising previously taken-for-granted assumptions about the social world. What should happen, though, is that sociologists ought not to be dismissive of happiness as an area of inquiry in its own right. It already has an implicit place in many sociological studies; those that explore society's pathologies, such as inequality or suffering, contain an – often unspoken – assumption that the alternative to such a pathology is a happier state, and that this is what such injustices prevent people from realising. Researching happiness in and of itself (rather than acknowledging it as simply a desired 'end point' of negative processes) can offer sociologists a clearer insight into what is actually meant by such 'alternatives'.

The profile of happiness should also be raised in sociology because of the central place that happiness occupies in society. The public are continually advised by the media and by advertisements that they should pursue happiness through the consumption of particular goods and services. Schools, colleges and universities are increasingly assuring their pupils and students that their happiness and well-being is paramount (Ecclestone and Hayes, 2009); indeed, universities are now ranked according to how satisfied students feel with their courses, using data from the United Kingdom's National Student Survey (National Student Survey, 2014). Furthermore, many organisations and workplaces are placing ever more emphasis upon the emotional well-being of employees (see NICE, 2014). Therefore, happiness is a major preoccupation for many people; not only it is something that almost everybody strives to achieve, but its promotion and promise is something that people are exposed to on a very regular basis. It should surely, then, be sociologists' duty to understand something that is so central to people's daily lives.

Appendix 1: Respondent Profiles

The details provided here were given to me by respondents at the time that they were interviewed. All were asked to rate their happiness on an 11-point scale (where 0 is 'extremely unhappy' and 10 is 'extremely happy') in answer to the question 'Taking all things together, how happy would you say you are?' prior to the start of their interview. This is a question that has been included in a range of large-scale government surveys. All names have been changed.

Alan (male) is 48 and works in human resources. He is married and has three teenage stepsons. He gets most of his happiness from social events with friends. He rated himself as four out of ten on the happiness scale. He was interviewed in his own home.

Alex (male) is 25 and works as a family support worker for a poverty charity. He is currently single. He feels most happy when he feels that he can express exactly who he is. He rated himself as six out of ten on the happiness scale. He was interviewed in his own home.

Beth (female) is 23 and is unemployed. She is currently single and shares a flat with a friend. She feels at her happiest when with friends and family, though she would feel a happier if she found work. She rated herself as five out of ten on the happiness scale, and she was interviewed in her own home.

Chloe (female) is 26 and is an actress. She is currently single and gets most of her happiness from progression in her acting career. She claims to be a 'big self-helper' and likes to 'work' at her happiness and take control of it, and it is for this reason that she feels quite happy. She rated herself as seven out of ten on the happiness scale. She was interviewed in her own home.

Chris (male) is 46 and is unemployed. He was born in Canada and has lived in the United Kingdom for seven months. He is separated from his partner and has a six-year-old son. He rated himself as six out of ten on the happiness scale, and whilst he gets a lot of happiness from living in London, he also feels that being unemployed has lowered his self-esteem. He was interviewed in his own home.

Danielle (female) is 26 and works as a trainee solicitor. She has a boyfriend and says that she is happier when she is in a relationship than when she is single. Her career is also an important source of happiness for her. She rated herself as seven out of ten on the happiness scale, and she was interviewed at her place of work.

Denise (female) is 46 and is an education welfare officer in a secondary school. She is a single mother and lives with her 17-year-old son, who is a big part of what makes her happy. She rated herself as eight out of ten on the happiness scale and feels that things are good at the moment as she has control over where her life is going (as compared to last year when she had some health problems). She was interviewed in her own home.

Eileen (female) is 63 and is a retired saleswoman. She has two sons, who are a major source of her happiness, and she lost her partner to cancer four years ago. She is very active in fundraising for a national cancer charity. She feels quite happy because she is due to shortly become a grandmother. She rated herself as eight out of ten on the happiness scale. She was interviewed in her own home.

Gillian (female) is 45 and works as an administrator for a law centre. She has no children and has a partner whom she does not live with. She identifies herself as a socialist and feels that it is the structure of society that is the cause of most people's unhappiness. She rated herself as seven out of ten on the happiness scale and feels that she is quite happy and has fewer problems than most other people she knows. She was interviewed at her place of work.

Helen (female) is 77 and is a retired nurse. She has never been married and is a practicing Christian. She gets a lot of happiness from her religious beliefs as these help to know where she will go after she passes away. She feels quite happy at the moment, although she feels, like many other respondents, that happiness is something that one cannot have all the time, but that rather comes in 'bursts'. She rated herself as seven out of ten on the happiness scale, and she was interviewed in her own home.

Laurence (male) is 65 and is retired after working for many years at a well-known historic building in London. He identifies himself as gay and had a long-term partner whom he lost to cancer some years ago. He would feel happier if he felt accepted in the world he lives in, and seen as an individual. He felt unable to rate himself on the happiness scale and claimed that his happiness levels fluctuate too quickly. He was interviewed in his own home.

Linda (female) is 65 and is a retired teacher. She is divorced and has a son and a daughter who both have children of their own. Spending time with her family, and particularly her grandchildren, is a major source of happiness for her. She feels that she is a naturally positive and an optimistic person. She rated herself as eight out of ten on the happiness scale. She was interviewed in her own home.

Lizzie (female) is 25 and works as a press and marketing officer for central government. She was born in New Zealand and has lived in the United Kingdom for a number of years. She is currently single and lives in a shared house with friends. She gets a lot of happiness from her work and is particularly happy with her recent career progression, but also feels that things would be better if she were in a relationship. She rated herself as eight out of ten on the happiness scale, and she was interviewed in her own home.

Mark (male) is 41 and works as an LGBT (Lesbian, Gay, Bisexual and Transgender) project coordinator for a national charity. He identifies himself as gay, and is single. He hopes to gain happiness from meeting his 'Mr Right'. He rated himself as seven out of ten on the happiness scale. He was interviewed in his own home.

Martin (male) is 32 and works as a lawyer. He is in a long-term relationship, and his girlfriend lives in New York. His relationship is a big source of happiness for him, although the distance also makes him feel frustrated. He also gets happiness from progression in his career, although he does not feel that he is progressing as much as he would like. He rated himself as six out of ten on the happiness scale, and he was interviewed in his own home.

Maureen (female) is 80 and has never worked. Her husband lives in a residential care home, and she has two sons, one of whom passed away several years ago, a daughter and several grandchildren. Her family's welfare is the most important thing in her life, and her happiness is often determined by the extent to which they are happy. One of the happiest times in her life was when her children were growing up. She rated herself as six out of ten on the happiness scale and was interviewed in her own home.

Nick (male) is 25 and is an actor. He has a girlfriend whom he does not live with, and gets most of his happiness from challenges in his work both in acting and television writing. He feels that happiness is not something that lasts forever, but that it is something which is in a constant state of 'flux'. He rated himself as seven out of ten on the happiness scale; he feels happy at the moment, although he also feels that he could also be happier as he still needs to achieve more in life. He was interviewed in his own home.

Sophie (female) is 22 and works as a receptionist. She is single and shares a flat with a friend. She enjoys helping others, and although she feels quite happy, she feels that a career change to something more fulfilling, as well as possibly finding a new relationship could increase her happiness further. She rated herself as six out of ten on the happiness scale, and she was interviewed in her own home.

Tom (male) is 25 and works part-time as an administration assistant for a charity. He is currently single and lives with his parents. He suffers from low self-esteem and would feel happier if he had a full-time job that was better paid and in which had more responsibility. He would also like to be able to afford to live independently. He rated himself as six out of ten on the happiness scale, and he was interviewed in his own home.

Appendix 2: Interview Questions

- What would you say makes you most happy in life?
- What do you think happiness is?
- Do you think that happiness is something that everyone wants to achieve? Or is it different for different people? Why do you think this is?
- Do you think that the idea of 'happiness' might have changed over time or over history?
- And do you think the idea of 'happiness' might be different across cultures?
- Do you feel happy at the moment? Why or why not?
- Would you say that happiness is a short-term, fleeting feeling or a longer-lasting state?
- Who is the happiest person you know, and why?
- If you could be given anything to make you feel happy/happier right now, what would it be?
- A lot of people take anti-depressants or see therapists and counsellors in order to feel happy these days. What do you think of this?
- Some people think that we need money and a lot of possessions in order to be truly happy. Would you say you agree with this?
- Do you think one needs to have good relationships with friends and family in order to be happy?
- To what extent do you think health is important for happiness and emotional well-being?
- Some might say that religion makes people happier – do you think this is true?
- How important do you think being in or falling in love is for feeling happy?
- Have you ever been in love? Did it make you happy? In what way(s)? What feelings did you experience?
- [If no] Would you like to?
- Do you think that sexual relationships are an important aspect of a happy life? Why? In what ways?

Bibliography

Action for Happiness. (2014). *Action for Happiness: About Us*. http://www
.actionforhappiness.org/about-us [accessed 25 April 2014].

Ahmed, S. (2010). *The Promise of Happiness*. Durham, Duke University Press.

Aristotle. (350 BC/1998). *The Nicomachean Ethics*, translated by D. Ross.
Oxford, Oxford University Press.

Barbalet, J. M. (Ed.) (2002). *Emotions and Sociology*. Oxford, Blackwell.

Barthes, R. (1978). *A Lover's Discourse*. New York, Hill and Wang.

Bartram, D. (2012). 'Elements of a sociological contribution to happiness
studies.' *Sociology Compass*. 6(8): 644–656.

Bauer, R. A. (1966). *Social Indicators*. London, Cambridge, MA, MIT Press.

Bauman, Z. (2000). *Liquid Modernity*. Cambridge, Polity.

Bauman, Z. (2001). *The Individualised Society*. Cambridge, Polity.

Bauman, Z. (2008). *The Art of Life*. Cambridge, Polity.

Beattie, M. (1992). *Codependent No More: How to Stop Controlling Others and
Start Caring for Yourself*. Minnesota, Hazelden.

Beck, U. (1992). *Risk Society: Towards a New Modernity*. London, Sage.

Beck, U. and Beck-Gernsheim, E. (1995). *The Normal Chaos of Love*. Cambridge,
Polity.

Beck, U. and Beck-Gernsheim, E. (2001). *Individualization: Institutionalized
Individualism and Its Social and Political Consequences*. London, Sage.

Bellah, R. N. (1985). *Habits of the Heart: Individualism and Commitment in
American Life*. Berkeley, University of California Press.

Bendelow, G. and Williams, S. (Eds.) (1998). *Emotions in Social Life: Critical
Themes and Contemporary Issues*. London, Routledge.

Bentham, J. (1789/2007). *The Principles of Morals and Legislation*. Mineola, NY,
Dover Publications.

Bourdieu, P. (1986). *Distinction*, translated by R. Nice. London, Routledge and
Kegan Paul.

Budgeon, S. (2008) 'Couple culture and the production of singleness.'
Sexualities. 11(3): 301–325.

Carr-West, J. (2014) *Council Matchmaking: Should Councils Help Us Make Friends?* http://www.theguardian.com/local-government-network/2014/mar/
31/council-matchmaking-relationships-wellbeing [accessed 25 April 2014].

Csikszentmihalyi, M. and Hunter, J. (2003). 'Happiness in everyday life: The
uses of experience sampling.' *Journal of Happiness Studies*. 4(2): 185–199.

Di Tella, R., MacCulloch, R. and Oswald, A. J. (2003). 'The macroeconomics of
happiness.' *Review of Economics and Statistics*. 85(4): 809–27.

Durkheim, E. (1912/1961). *The Elementary Forms of the Religious Life*. New York,
Collier.

Easterlin, R. A. (2001). 'Income and happiness: Towards a unified theory.' *The Economic Journal*. 111: 465–484.

Easterlin, R. (1974). 'Does economic growth improve the human lot? Some empirical evidence.' In P. A. David (Ed.), *Nations and Households in Economic Growth: Essays in Honour of Moses Abramovitz*. London, New York, Academic Press, pp. 89–125.

Ecclestone, K. and Hayes, D. (2009). *The Dangerous Rise of Therapeutic Education*. Abingdon, Routledge.

Ehrenreich, B. (2010). *Smile or Die: How Positive Thinking Fooled American and the World*. London, Granta Books.

Ekman, P. and Cordaro, D. (2011). 'What is meant by calling emotions basic?' *Emotion Review*. 3(4): 364–370.

Fearn, H. (2014). *Happiness Is Good for your Health, So What Are Councils Doing about It?* http://www.theguardian.com/local-government-network/2014/apr/18/what-should-be-included-in-public-health [accessed 25 April 2014].

Foucault, M. (1972). *The Archaeology of Knowledge*. London, Routledge.

Foucault, M. (1977). *Discipline and Punish: The Birth of the Prison*. London, Allen Lane.

Foucault, M. (1982). 'The subject and power.' In H. Dreyfus and P. Rabinow (Eds.), *Michel Foucault: Beyond Structuralism and Hermeneutics*. Chicago, University of Chicago Press, pp. 208–227.

Foucault, M. (1986). *The History of Sexuality Volume 3: The Care of the Self*. New York, Vintage Books.

Foucault, M. (1988). 'Technologies of the self.' In L. H. Martin, H. Gutman and P. H. Hutton (Eds.), *Technologies of the Self*. London, Tavistock, pp. 16–49.

Foucault, M. (1991). 'Politics and the study of discourse.' In G. Burchell, C. Gordon and P. Miller (Eds.), *The Foucault Effect: Studies in Governmentality: With Two Lectures by and an Interview with Michel Foucault*. Chicago, University of Chicago Press, pp. 53–72.

Frey, B. S. and Stutzer, A. (2002). *Happiness and Economics: How the Economy and Institutions Affect Human Well-being*. Princeton, Princeton University Press.

Fromm, E. (1942). *The Fear of Freedom*. London, Routledge.

Furedi, F. (2004). *Therapy Culture: Cultivating Vulnerability in an Uncertain Age*. London, Routledge.

Gardner, J. and Oswald, A. (2002). *Is It Money or Marriage That Keeps People Alive?* Mimeo, University of Warwick.

Giddens, A. (1991). *Modernity and Self-Identity: Self and Society in the Late Modern Age*. Cambridge, Polity Press.

Goffman, E. (1959). *The Presentation of Self in Everyday Life*. London, Penguin.

Goleman, D. (1996). *Emotional Intelligence: Why It Can Matter More Than IQ*. London, Bloomsbury.

Greco, M. and Stenner, P. (Eds.) (2008). *Emotions: A Social Science Reader*. Abingdon, Routledge.

Hazleden, R. (2003). 'Love yourself: The relationship of the self with itself in popular self-help texts.' *Journal of Sociology*. 39(4): 413–428.

Helliwell, J. F. (2003). 'How's life? Combining individual and national variables to explain subjective well-being.' *Economic Modelling*. 20(2): 331–360.

Helliwell, J. F. and Putnam, R. D. (2004) 'The social context of well-being.' *Philosophical Transactions of the Royal Society B*. 359: 1435–1446.

Hill, N. (2002). *The Law of Success in Sixteen Lessons*. New York, United Holdings Group.

Hochschild, A. R. (1979). 'Emotion work, feeling rules and social structure.' *American Journal of Sociology*. 85(3): 551–575.

Hochschild, A. R. (1983). *The Managed Heart: Commercialization of Human Feeling*. Berkeley, University of California Press.

Hochschild, A. R. (1998). 'The sociology of emotion as a way of seeing.' In G. Bendelow and S. Williams (Eds.), *Emotions in Social Life: Critical Themes and Contemporary Issues*. London, Routledge, pp. 3–16.

Holden, R. (2007). *Happiness Now! Timeless Wisdom for Feeling Good Fast*. Carlsbad, CA, Hay House.

Illouz, E. (2007). *Cold Intimacies: The Making of Emotional Capitalism*. Cambridge, Polity.

Illouz, E. (2008). *Saving the Modern Soul: Therapy, Emotions and the Culture of Self-Help*. Berkeley, University of California Press.

Jackson, S. (1993). 'Even sociologists fall in love: An exploration in the sociology of emotions.' *Sociology*. 27(1): 201–220.

Jackson, S. (1999). *Heterosexuality in Question*. London, Sage.

Jeffers, S. (1997). *Feel the Fear and Do It Anyway: How to Turn your Fear and Indecision into Confidence and Action*. London, Vermilion.

Johnson, P. J. (2005). *Love, Heterosexuality and Society*. London, Routledge.

Kahneman, D., Diener, E. and Schwarz, N. (1999). *Well-Being: The Foundations of Hedonic Psychology*. New York, Russell Sage Foundation.

Kahneman, D., Krueger, A. B., Schkade, D. A., Schwarz, N. and Stone, A. A. (2004). 'A survey method for characterising daily life experience: The day reconstruction method.' *Science*. 306(5702): 1776–1780.

Kant, I. (1785/1981). *Grounding for the Metaphysics of Morals*, translated by J. W. Ellington. Indianapolis, IN, Hackett.

Kemper, T. D. (1984). 'Power, status and emotions: A sociological contribution to a psychophysiological domain.' In K. Scherer and P. Ekman (Eds.), *Approaches to Emotion*. Hillsdale, NJ, Lawrence Erlbaum, pp. 396–383.

Kitayama, S. and Markus, H. R. (2000). 'The pursuit of happiness and the realization of sympathy: Cultural patterns of self, social relations, and well-being.' In E. Diener and E. M. Suh (Eds.), *Culture and Subjective Well-Being*. Cambridge, MA, MIT Press, pp. 113–162.

Kotchemidova, C. (2005). 'From good cheer to "Drive-By Smiling": A social history of cheerfulness.' *Journal of Social History*. 39(1): 5–37.

Langford, W. (1999). *Revolutions of the Heart: Gender, Power and the Delusions of Love*. London, Routledge.

Lasch, C. (1979). *The Culture of Narcissism: American Life in an Age of Diminishing Expectations*. New York, W.W. Norton and Co.

Lawler, S. (2005). 'Disgusted subjects: The making of middle-class identities.' *The Sociological Review*. 53(3): 429–446.

Layard, R. (2011). *Happiness: Lessons from a New Science*, 2nd ed. London, Penguin.

Leppamaki, S., Partonen, T. and Lonnqvist, J. (2002). 'Bright-light exposure combined with physical exercise elevates mood.' *Journal of Affective Disorders*. 72(2): 139–144.

Lumie. (2014). *Guide to Seasonal Affective Disorder (SAD)*. http://www.lumie. com/blogs/quick-guides/6212116-sad-seasonal-affective-disorder-and-winter-blues [accessed 18 September 2014].

Lupton, D. (1998). *The Emotional Self: A Sociocultural Exploration*. London, Sage.

Marx, K. (1867/1999). *Capital*. Oxford, Oxford University Press.

Marx, K. and Engels, F. (1988). *Economic and Philosophic Manuscripts of 1844 and the Communist Manifesto*, translated by M. Milligan. Amherst, NY, Prometheus Books.

Mayer, J. D. and Salovey, P. (1993). 'The intelligence of emotional intelligence.' *Intelligence*. 17: 433–442.

Mead, G. H. (1934). *Mind, Self and Society: From the Standpoint of a Social Behaviorist*. Chicago, University of Chicago Press.

Mill, J. S. (1863/2001). *Utilitarianism*, 2nd revised ed. Indianapolis, Hackett Publishing.

National Student Survey. (2014). *The National Student Survey 2014*. http:// www.thestudentsurvey.com/ [accessed 25 April 2014].

NICE (2014). *Promoting Mental Wellbeing at Work*. http://www.nice.org.uk/ PH22 [accessed 25 April 2014].

Office for National Statistics (2014). *Measuring National Well-Being*. http:// www.ons.gov.uk/ons/guide-method/user-guidance/well-being/index.html [accessed 25 April 2014].

Oswald, A. (1997). 'Happiness and economic performance.' *The Economic Journal*. 107: 1815–1831.

Pahl, R. (2005). 'Are all communities, communities in the mind?' *Sociological Review Monograph*. 4(53): 621–40.

Plato (380 BC/1998). *Republic*, translated by R. Waterfield. Oxford, Oxford University Press.

Richardson, J. (2014). *Happiness and Well-Being Trump Material Growth*. http:// www.theguardian.com/sustainable-business/blog/happiness-wellbeing -bhutan-gus-odonnell-policy [accessed 25 April 2014].

Rieff, P. (1966). *The Triumph of the Therapeutic: Uses of Faith after Freud*. New York, Harper and Row.

Rimke, H. M. (2000). 'Governing citizens through self-help literature.' *Cultural Studies*. 14(1): 61–78.

Rose, N. (1996). *Inventing Our Selves: Psychology, Power and Personhood*. Cambridge, Cambridge University Press.

Savage, M. (2000). *Class Analysis and Social Transformation*. Buckingham, Open University Press.

Schwartz, B. (2005). *The Paradox of Choice: Why More Is Less*. New York, Harper Perennial.

Seligman, M. E. P. (2002). *Authentic Happiness: Using the New Positive Psychology to Realize Your Potential for Lasting Fulfillment*. New York, Free Press.

Shaw, I. and Taplin, S. (2007). 'Happiness and mental health policy: A sociological critique.' *Journal of Mental Health*. 16(3): 359–373.

Shott, S. (1979). 'Emotion and social life: A symbolic interactionist analysis.' *American Journal of Sociology*. 84(6): 1317–1334.

Simmel, G. (1903). 'The metropolis and mental life.' In K. H. Wolff (Ed.) (1950), *The Sociology of Georg Simmel*. New York, Free Press, pp. 409–424.

Skeggs, B. (1997). *Formations of Class and Gender: Becoming Respectable*. London, Sage.

Skeggs, B. (2004). *Class, Self, Culture*. London, Routledge.

Smart, B. (2010). *Consumer Society: Critical Issues and Environmental Consequences*. London, Sage.

Stevens, T. G. (2010). *You Can Choose To Be Happy: 'Rise Above' Anxiety, Anger and Depression*. Palm Desert, CA, Wheeler Sutton Publishers.

Thin, N. (2012). *Social Happiness: Theory into Policy and Practice*. Bristol, Policy.

Time to Change (2014). *Who Are We?* http://www.time-to-change.org.uk/about-us/what-is-time-to-change [accessed 25 April 2014].

Turner, J. H. and Stets, J. E. (2005). *The Sociology of Emotions*. New York, Cambridge University Press.

Vedral, J. (1994). *Get Rid of Him!* New York, Warner Books.

Veenhoven, R. (2004). 'Happiness as an aim in public policy: The greatest happiness principle.' In A. Linley and S. Joseph (Eds.), *Positive Psychology in Practice*. Hoboken, NJ, John Wiley and Sons, pp. 658–768.

Weber, M. (1904/2002). *The Protestant Ethic and the Spirit of Capitalism*, translated by P. Baehr, G. C. Wells. New York, Penguin Classics.

Wellman, B. (1979). 'The community question.' *American Journal of Sociology*. 84: 1201–31.

Williams, M. and Penman, D. (2011). *Mindfulness: A Practical Guide to Finding Peace in a Frantic World*. London, Piatkus.

Wright, K. (2008). 'Theorizing therapeutic culture: Past influences, future directions.' *Journal of Sociology*. 44(4): 321–336.

Index

Printed and bound by CPI Group (UK) Ltd, Croydon, CR0 4YY